The Deals of
Warren Buffett

Despite holding positions of Professor of Investment and Professor of Corporate Finance, Glen Arnold concluded that academic life was not nearly as much fun (nor as intellectually stimulating) as making money in the markets. As a wealthy investor in his fifties, he now spends most of his time running his equity portfolio and a property development company from an office in the heart of rural Leicestershire, far from the noise of the City of London.

His main research focus explores the question, 'What works in investment?', drawing on the ideas of the great investors, academic discoveries and corporate strategic analysis – see www.glen-arnold-investments.co.uk. While he used to teach on this subject in the City, he would now rather concentrate on actual investment analysis, but does explain his investment choices and discusses investment ideas at newsletters.advfn.com/deepvalueshares.

He is the author of the UK's bestselling investment book and bestselling corporate finance textbook.

Also by Glen Arnold

The Deals of Warren Buffett

Volume 1, The First $100m

Glen Arnold

HARRIMAN HOUSE

HARRIMAN HOUSE LTD
18 College Street
Petersfield
Hampshire
GU31 4AD
GREAT BRITAIN
Tel: +44 (0)1730 233870
Email: enquiries@harriman-house.com
Website: www.harriman-house.com

First published in Great Britain in 2017
Copyright © Glen Arnold

Hardback ISBN: 978-0-85719-603-3
eBook ISBN: 978-0-85719-604-0

British Library Cataloguing in Publication Data
A CIP catalogue record for this book can be obtained from the British Library.

Contents

Foreword by Lawrence Cunningham

I have studied Berkshire Hathaway for more than two decades as it blossomed from a noted but niche player into a magnetic force with a worldwide following numbering in the millions. As the promulgator of a compelling philosophy of investing and business, Berkshire now boasts an entire ecosystem of people and ideas predicated upon rational capital allocation and corporate structure. Investors, managers, and scholars alike sustain this vast fruitful field of human endeavor in selecting investments, operating businesses, and producing articles, books, and conferences.

In 1996, I hosted a symposium featuring Warren Buffett and his letters to Berkshire shareholders, which I rearranged thematically and published as *The Essays of Warren Buffett*. At the time, Buffett was known in financial circles, and had a sizable and loyal following among Berkshire shareholders, but was not a household name. A handful of books about Buffett and Berkshire appeared around this time, led by Robert Hagstrom's *The Warren Buffett Way* about investing, along with a biography by Roger Lowenstein.

During the ensuing two decades, Warren became famous and Berkshire a promoter and progenitor of many luminaries in business, investment, and scholarship. Warren popularized and transformed value investing from a marginal backwater to a mainstay of the field; he perfected autonomous decentralized management that others are beginning to follow; and he is far along in a process of donating virtually his entire wealth of some US$75 billion to charitable institutions. Today, nearly 40,000 attend Berkshire's annual meeting, all three of the books I mentioned above and a dozen others have become big international sellers, and few people are better known or more admired on the world stage than Warren Buffett.

Books in the genre span the topics Buffett has addressed so adeptly, which may be organized, as *The Essays* are, into such subjects as accounting, finance, governance, investing, takeovers, taxes, and valuation. With Buffett's work spanning more than a half-century, efforts are underway to segment these topics by era, such as:

- early Berkshire (through its 1978 consolidating reorganization);

- Berkshire as primarily an investor in stocks (1978–2000); and

- Berkshire as largely a conglomerate of diverse wholly owned businesses (since then).

It is the breadth and depth of Buffett's contributions to knowledge in these areas, and the sheer length of time over which he has led this company, that induces so many analysts and authors to dissect Buffett's work and Berkshire's practices. As the story still goes strong, observers of the Buffett-Berkshire scene can readily learn from their latest decisions and acquisitions.

What's more, it remains possible, despite prodigious written coverage, to gain insight from retellings of Berkshire and Buffett's past, particularly the early days. My recent book, *Berkshire Beyond Buffett*, is part of such a trend, a look back at how Berkshire's corporate culture formed and ahead to how that culture will sustain Berkshire long after Warren takes his leave.

Glen Arnold's book offers a similar vantage point, with a very specific focus on Buffett's formative investing experiences. By returning to Buffett's earliest investments – such as GEICO and See's Candies – and adding a contemporary understanding,

Professor Arnold contributes useful history and lucid investment analysis, providing context, color, and lessons from Warren's school days through Berkshire circa 1978.

Buffett is fond of aphorisms, and a favorite source is the Spanish philosopher, George Santyana, who warned that "those who do not remember the past are condemned to repeat it." Buffett's letters routinely identify the rationales for his investments and highlight both those that were rational and those where errors in reasoning or logic occurred. In Professor Arnold's book, these lessons are extracted and collated in sharp, clear prose.

Buffett is also fond of saying he hopes to be remembered most not as an investor, businessman, or philanthropist, but as a teacher. In *The Investment Deals of Warren Buffett*, readers can sense the teacher in Professor Arnold, as he lays out thoughtful block lessons in an engaging sequence. All but the most expert aficionados of the Berkshire saga will find valuable knowledge here.

Every owner of a physical copy of this edition of

The Deals of Warren Buffett

can download the eBook for free direct from us
at Harriman House, in a format that can be read
on any eReader, tablet or smartphone.

Simply head to:

ebooks.harriman-house.com/dealsofwb1

to get your free eBook now.

Preface

What this book covers

Starting out with $120 of savings as an 11-year-old in 1941, it took the world's greatest investor, Warren Buffett, around four decades to make his first $100m. This book tracks the deals he made in this 37-year period, explains the reasoning behind each key investment, and shows how he accumulated wealth from the start of his career onwards.

Without much of an idea about share investing at the beginning, Buffett had to develop his investment philosophy, and learn through success and failure how to select companies worth backing. This book tells the story of how Buffett's investment philosophy was developed, and provides lessons for today's investors.

It was not all plain sailing for Buffett, with many mistakes made along the way. There were long periods of frustration mixed in with the triumphs. The fact that Buffett made errors is quite reassuring for other investors. It is comforting to know that a person who eventually made billions was also prone to errors – it helps us to be resilient in the face of our own setbacks. The biggest error of all is to assume investors have to be flawless at all times. Psychologically, investors have to prepare for many wrong turns and knocks, and then bounce back. And it is always worth bearing in mind that we can learn from other people's mistakes as well as our own; who better to learn from than Buffett casting judgement on his own errors?

With the focus of this book being on analysing investment deals, I devote little attention to Buffett's personal life. If you are looking for that sort of autobiographical story, then this book is not for you. If, however, you want to become a better investor and understand how it is possible for someone to make large sums of money by following sound investing principles, then read on.

Who this book is for

This book is for investors who want to learn, or be prompted to bring again to the front of the mind, the vital rules for successful investment. The learning process is set in the framework of a series of fascinating case studies about Warren Buffett's investment deals.

How the book is structured

The book follows Buffett's journey to his first $100m. We start with the first stock market investment Buffett made when he was still a boy and review the history of 22 of his investment deals in total. Part 2 is arranged as a series of chapters that focus on these deals in turn. You can dip in and read about particular deals that take your interest if you wish, but I would encourage you to read chronologically at first, to achieve an understanding of how Buffett developed as an investor. Each story in the journey has useful lessons for us today.

Not every investment Buffett made over this 37-year period is described – that would have led to an excessively long book. Only the most impactful case studies, on Buffett's wealth and on his philosophy, have been chosen for analysis.

Before I begin to look at the series of deals, Part 1 includes two introductory chapters that are important for getting the most out of the rest of the book. The first provides a concise summary of the investment deals covered in Part 2. In the second chapter, I examine how Benjamin Graham influenced Buffett's investment philosophy.

A note on common abbreviations: I use the abbreviation BPL to refer to Buffett Partnership Ltd, which was Warren Buffett's investment partnership in the early part of his career. In researching and writing this book, I have drawn quite widely on Buffett's letters to his partners in the BPL. These letters are readily available on the internet. I also use the abbreviation BH for Berkshire Hathaway.

Introduction

The origins of the book lie in a period about four years ago when I took the big decision to stop other activities to permit full concentration on stock market investing. This meant giving up a tenured professorship, ceasing lucrative teaching in the City of London and, ironically, pulling back sharply on writing books.

As part of my new full-time investment process, to create a record of the logical process I went through to select shares, I wrote short blogs laying out my analysis on a simple free website. I found it galvanising to be forced to express clearly and publically the reasons why I had allocated capital in a particular way. And besides, my memory is so bad that I needed a way to recall a few months down the line my reasons for the investments I had made.

I was later asked by the investment website ADVFN if I would like to write on their newsletter page. I accepted and one strand of my writing became a series of articles about the investment deals of Warren Buffett. It is from those articles that this book has been created.

The 'Why?' question

You might think that Buffett has already been covered in hundreds of published volumes and there is nothing new to say, but having read much of this literature myself I was left unsatisfied. Many other writers on Buffett address what he invested in and how much he made from it. But I wanted to know why. What were the special characteristics about the companies Buffett chose that made them stand out? Was it in the balance sheet numbers, the profit history, the strategic positioning and/or the qualities of management? I wanted to know the detail. How did Buffett go from step to step, from having virtually no money to being very rich?

For each of his major steps I tried to get to greater depth on the why angle. For each investment this required fresh investigation, using many sources. My priority was to focus on analytical material about the companies Buffett selected and I did not dedicate much time to Buffett's personal life, which has been thoroughly covered elsewhere. Accordingly you will not find much about Buffett's personal life in this book.

There were dozens of key investment deals to cover and each needed a full analysis. Justice would not be done if they were squeezed into one book and so it made sense to stop the first volume at the point where Buffett reached the major milestone of $100m net worth, and when he had consolidated his investments in one holding company, Berkshire Hathaway. He did this in 1978, aged 48, and that is where this first book in the series ends.

The Buffett connection

My eyes were opened to the profundity of Buffett's ideas many years ago. Naturally, I became a shareholder in Berkshire Hathaway, and regularly visited Omaha for the Berkshire Hathaway AGM.

My favourite anecdote from my visits to Omaha is the one where I, and I alone, definitely forced Buffett to give away $40bn. You may think Buffett is strong-minded and couldn't possibly be swayed by a visiting Brit. But I know differently – and I know I'm right!

It happened in 2006 when Bill Gates (this is serious name dropping now!) was with Buffett. Gates is a close friend of

Buffett and a director of Berkshire Hathaway. I thanked Gates for the great work he and his wife Melinda were doing with their Foundation – I was most effusive, perhaps a little over the top.

Then I turned to a listening Buffett standing next to Gates and said, "Thank you for all you are doing for Berkshire Hathaway shareholders." I don't know what it was, but my voice did not convey quite as much excitement about Buffett's achievements as it had about Gates'.

Would you believe it? In a matter of weeks Buffett announced that he was going to hand over to the Bill & Melinda Gates Foundation the vast majority of his fortune, to be used for charitable purposes around the world. Clearly, Buffett had deeply pondered why this Brit was less impressed by Berkshire Hathaway, his creation, than by the Gates Foundation, his friends' creation. He took action to do something about that.

That's my story and I'm sticking to it until the day I die!

I hope you enjoy reading how Buffett made his first $100m.

Glen Arnold,
summer 2017

PART 1.
SETTING THE SCENE

The Warren Buffett Story

It is helpful to begin the book with a quick summary of the story so far, in the investing career of the greatest living investor. This lays the foundation for the exploration of his investment deals that follows.

Youth and partnerships

A teenage Buffett read Benjamin Graham's book, *The Intelligent Investor*, in 1949. He later enrolled on Graham's Columbia University course and subsequently worked as a security analyst for him from 1954–6. Benjamin Graham's ideas formed the foundation for Buffett's success.

As well as learning a great deal from Graham at this time, Buffett made some spectacular investment deals, such as the 48% gain in a few months from his GEICO shares when 21 years old (Investment 2), and the Rockwood chocolate chip bonanza, in which the 24-year-old Buffett more than doubled his investment, making $13,000 to add to his growing fund (Investment 5).

On returning home to Omaha, Nebraska, following Graham's retirement, the 25-year-old Buffett set up an investment partnership with seven relatives and friends, with Buffett taking the investing decisions – there was only $105,000 available to invest at the outset.

Year after year the partnership's returns far exceeded those of the broad stock market, as Buffett found bargain after bargain, such as Sanborn Maps sitting on net assets per share worth much more than its share price – partners made about a 50% return on that investment, when Buffett was 29 years old (Investment 6).

Other investors observed what Buffett was doing and wanted him to invest their money, so he set up other partnerships. He found some wonderful companies temporarily out of favour with Wall Street, such as American Express (a trebling in share price for Buffett – Investment 8) and Walt Disney (a 55% return – Investment 9).

Between the start of the partnership phase of Buffett's investing career (first full year 1957) and near its end in 1968, the Dow Jones Industrial Average index (DJIA, or simply Dow) grew by 185.7%, but a dollar invested with Buffett went up by 2,610.6%. Yes, each $1,000 invested in 1957 became worth $27,106 within 12 years. After Buffett's fees a typical partner would have over $15,000. In contrast, each $1,000 invested in the Dow in 1957 increased to only $2,857.

Chart A illustrates the performance of Buffett's Partnership before and after fees, and the Dow Jones index, over this period. Note that the various partnerships were brought together into one, Buffett Partnership Ltd (BPL), in 1962 – the performance figures for 1957–61 are consolidated from the range of partnerships, which were pretty similar.

What I'm about to tell you will seem more remarkable if I first state that today Berkshire Hathaway is the fourth largest US stock market listed company (after Apple, Alphabet and Microsoft), with a market capitalisation (total market value of its shares) of over $400bn and a share price of $245,000.

Chart A: Comparing the performance of the Dow Jones index and Warren Buffett's investment partnership (1957–68)

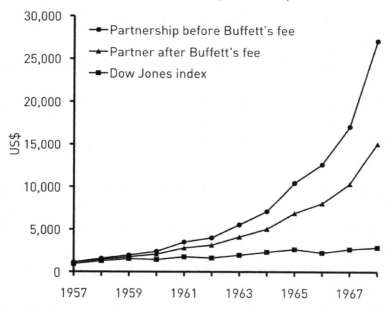

Berkshire Hathaway enters the scene

In 1962, Buffett used a portion of his partners' money to buy shares in a down-at-heel New England textile company, Berkshire Hathaway. The price of each share averaged $7.50 (no, I have not missed any zeros). It was loss-making. By May 1964, BPL held 7% of the shares of Berkshire Hathaway.

The dominant shareholder and executive of Berkshire Hathaway was Seabury Stanton. He made a deal with Buffett for Berkshire Hathaway to buy BPL's Berkshire Hathaway shares for $11.50 – 50% more than Warren had paid to acquire them. Then, Stanton thought he'd chisel Buffett. In a petty way, he pitched the formal offer at only $11.375. Buffett bristled at Stanton's behaviour and chose not to sell.

Instead, Buffett made what he later called "a monumentally stupid decision". It was plain for all to see that New England textile mills were going out of business as they rarely made profits; they had been hit by cheap imports. Berkshire Hathaway itself had closed most of its mills as it failed to compete. But Buffett was upset and so began to aggressively buy more shares in Berkshire Hathaway. (Great investors are not perfectly rational – they make mistakes, as all investors do.) By April 1965, BPL held 39% of Berkshire Hathaway and formally took control of the company, using one-quarter of the funds under Buffett's command to do so.

Buffett's self-confessed "childish behaviour" resulted in him having to organise "a terrible business". As a result of losses and share repurchases, at the end of 1964 Berkshire's balance sheet net worth was only $22m. It had no excess cash and $2.5m of debt (see Investment 10).

Buffett put strict limits on further investment in textile machinery and other assets. He gradually moved the capital of the original business to some very interesting areas. Because he was not a textiles man, more a capital allocator with a knowledge of many types of businesses, he was able to spot better investment opportunities than those people who were focused on only the textile industry.

In 1967, he made a great leap for Berkshire Hathaway by getting it to buy the insurance company National Indemnity in his home town of Omaha for $8.6m (see Investment 11). The key attraction of insurance companies for Buffett, apart from the possibility of making money by charging more for insurance policies than the total of claims payouts and administration costs, is the pile of cash (the float) sitting within the firm. This is created because policyholders pay upfront but the claims payouts occur later. This float could be invested by Buffett. He bought many more insurance companies over the years and made very good use of the floats (see Investments 17 and 22).

The National Indemnity acquisition was followed by another masterstroke: the purchase of a chain of branded candy stores in 1972 for $25m. Up to the time of writing, this business, See's Candies, has generated over £1.9bn for Berkshire Hathaway to invest elsewhere. And it is still pumping out money today (see Investment 20).

Chart B: Berkshire Hathaway performance: annual percentage return (1965–78)

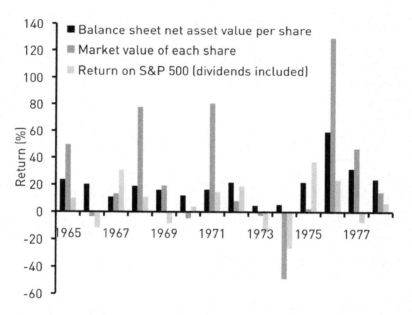

Source: Letter from the Chairman of Berkshire Hathaway (2016)

Many other brilliant investments were to follow, resulting in extraordinary growth for Berkshire, the once declining textile company. Between 1965 and 1978, the annual compound rate of growth of the S&P 500 was 4.63%. But for Berkshire the compound rate of growth in per share book value was 21%.

It is not until you see the effect of that differential on final dollar amounts that you really appreciate the truly stunning performance of Buffett. Whereas the S&P 500 rate of return resulted in a 1965 $1,000 investment being turned into $1,885 by December 1978, over those same 14 years a $1,000 investment in Berkshire Hathaway shares grew to be worth over $14,000. See Chart B for the annual growth in Berkshire's balance sheet value and the growth of its share price from 1965 until Buffett had made his first $100m in 1978.

Berkshire Hathaway has continued to outperform the S&P. Taking the whole period from January 1965 to December 2016, the annual compound rate of growth of the S&P 500 was 9.7%, but for Berkshire was more than double, at 20.8%. The S&P 500 rate of return resulted in a 1965 $1,000 investment being turned into $127,170 by December 2016, while over those same 52 years a $1,000 investment in Berkshire Hathaway shares grew to be worth almost $20m. See Chart C for the annual growth in Berkshire's balance sheet value and the growth of its share price over those years. I think we can safely say that Buffett has made amends for his "stupid decision" to buy Berkshire Hathaway!

That concludes my very broad sweep of how Warren Buffett made his money. Before we move on to look at the investment deals in more detail in Part 2, we need to understand the important role of the teachings of Benjamin Graham in Buffett's investment career. In the next section, I describe the influence that Graham had on Buffett, and how this guided Buffett's investment approach.

The Benjamin Graham school of practical investing

By 1950, aged 56, Benjamin Graham had already been through some pretty rough times on the stock market running small investment funds. Prior to the Wall Street Crash, Graham was a relatively cautious investor, but not cautious enough as the

Chart C: Berkshire Hathaway performance: annual percentage return (1979–2016)

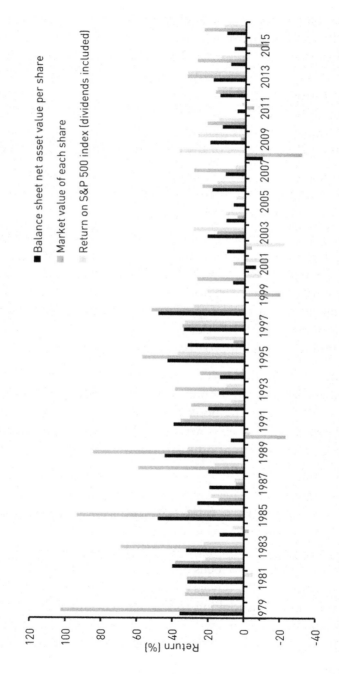

■ Balance sheet net asset value per share
Market value of each share
Return on S&P 500 index (dividends included)

Source: Letter from the Chairman of Berkshire Hathaway (2016)

downturn approached. Between 1929 and 1932, 70% of the $2.5m fund he was running for clients was lost or withdrawn. Graham was forced to reflect on what it is that makes an investor. He had experienced valuations made on projections of earnings made in optimistic mood. He had experienced buying in the hope of selling on to a greater fool who will pay even more because the price had gone up. He had experienced buying based on charts, tips, no real knowledge of the business, and insider knowledge.

These methods had all been shown wanting. The result of his soul-searching was the foundation of the value school of investing, which is so widely adhered to today.

To assist Graham in his thinking, and to pass on his knowledge, he taught a part-time course called Security Analysis at Columbia Business School. The first course was in 1927 (actually, temporarily, at the New York Institute of Finance), but I can imagine the intellectual depth increased in the early 1930s with forced pondering of the vexing questions raised by the failure of so many investment approaches in the Crash of 1929.

Together with David Dodd, a collaborator at Columbia, Graham set down his ideas in a book also called *Security Analysis*, first published in 1934. The book that the 19-year-old Buffett read, *The Intelligent Investor*, is a more concise version of his ideas. Among other important influences, it moved Buffett away from speculating to investing.

Following the 1929 Crash, many observers concluded that it was pointless assessing share value. After all, if in 1928 a share could be worth (according to the market price) $100 and 15 months later worth only $5, who was to know what the real value was? Far better, they said, was to focus on assessing the mood of other share buyers; whether other buyers think it will go up, and to try to buy before it does. This looking to the market, rather than looking to the company and its performance in serving its customers, is one distinguishing feature of speculators, as opposed to investors.

The definition of investment

With those features of speculation identified, we need a contrasting definition of investing. Graham and Dodd provided the following:

> "An investment operation is one which, upon thorough analysis, promises safety of principal and a satisfactory return. Operations not meeting these requirements are speculative."[1]

There are three essential elements here:

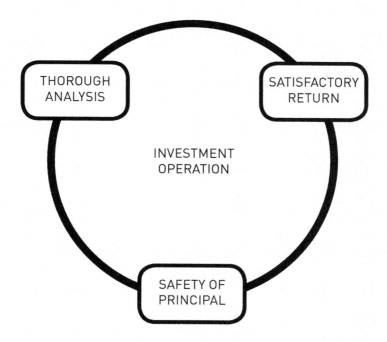

1. Thorough analysis

You are investing in a business; you will own a small portion of that business. Ask much the same questions you would ask if you were buying the whole of the business rather than just a small portion:

- What is the turnover and profit history?

- Does it have a good reputation with customers?

- Does it have lots of assets with few debts?

- What competition does it have?

- Are the managers competent and honest?

This type of analysis requires rationality, independence of mind and a critical examination of the facts. For Graham this analysis was primarily focused on the proven facts from the quantitative side. He recognised the importance of the qualitative, such as the power of a well-recognised brand or the quality of the managerial team, but his 1929 experience made him cautious about putting too much weight on his assessment of the business prospects and management's ability and integrity.

2. Safety of principal

It is very important to build in a margin of safety when buying shares, rather like the extra safety built into a road bridge. A bridge is not built to just about withstand historically recorded wind speeds and other loads; it is built to standards way beyond that.

Similarly, only buy shares when there is a large margin of safety between the purchase price and your calculation of intrinsic value. Think hard about the downside.

3. Satisfactory return

Don't aim to shoot the lights out. Don't get caught up in over-optimism or greed which will lead you down a path beyond your capabilities, or stretch the risk limits that you can stand.

The great irony

Remember the irony: great investors act with safety of principal in mind and aim only for a satisfactory rate of return. Yet, over the long run, they outperform those who take the path of higher risk.

Warren Buffett's other lessons from Graham

As well as this three-part definition of investing, Buffett also picked up other important lessons from Graham. He learned that returns depend on the investor's:

- knowledge
- experience
- temperament

The investor needs to understand the business world and how it works. Some grasp of accounting, finance and corporate strategy is essential, though this can be enhanced and developed over time. Having a curious mind is a prerequisite, but an investor does not have to develop the level of knowledge required purely from his own experience. A lot can be learned vicariously, from other's mistakes and successes.

Temperament is more important than IQ when it comes to being a good investor. Graham taught Buffett that the most intelligent people often make poor investors because they frequently lack the right mental approach. For example, if they are highly rational, they get frustrated at the irrationality in the market, and cannot figure a way of exploiting irrationality – they just see it as nuts. Also they can fall in love with their projections and predictions, thereby neglecting to build in a margin of safety. Other aspects of bad temperament for investors are the tendency to go with the crowd when it is panicking, or to become irrationally exuberant when everyone else is. Then, there are the people who can't help noticing others making money on some new idea for speculative selection or the latest whizz-bang technology and want some of the action. In short, the investor's own worst enemy is often herself.

Look at the facts

Graham rammed home to Buffett that he must understand the focus employed by other people in the markets if he wanted to outperform them. For example, many so-called investors were primarily concerned with expectations concerning the future, such as how many customers would sign up to the latest media product over the next ten years – something that could not be predicted with any degree of certainty. As a result of this poor focus, they would pay little heed to the more important details, such as the balance sheet, earnings history and price of the shares.

The lesson is not to become engrossed in the story of a business and ignore the real facts about it. It is extremely difficult to predict which of the story stocks will have a happy ending; which will be the dominant one in that market niche. And often there is no winner, at least not in terms of good returns on capital employed. Thus we must go along with what Graham said: "Analysis is concerned primarily with values which are supported by the facts and not those which depend largely upon expectations."[2]

As Buffett said about Graham:

> "[He] wasn't about brilliant investments and he wasn't about fads or fashion. He was about sound investing, and I think sound investing can make you very wealthy if you're not in too big of a hurry, and it never makes you poor, which is better."[3]

Buffett learned from Graham a method of communicating sophisticated investment principles in easy to remember parables. The Mr Market idea is a wonderful example and something we all need to be reminded about daily.

Graham told the following story. You are in a business partnership with Mr Market. You own 50%, the same as he. Every day Mr Market comes to you offering either to buy your half of the business or to sell his half to you. He is very obliging indeed – in fact he'll offer prices throughout the day. The thing is, Mr Market has moods. Some days he is very optimistic and offers you a very high price for your share of the business. At other times he is down in the dumps and just wants out – he will sell his half to you at a low price.

So, what you have to ask yourself is whether you should value your shares based on the prices that Mr Market is currently offering. I hope you would not. You will do your own analysis and compare your intrinsic value calculation with Mr Market's offer.

Learning points

1. **Follow sound investment principles**. The fundamental analytical approaches developed in the Graham and Dodd school of investing, both by them and their followers, are a good place to start. Find the right mentors, whether living or among the eminent dead.

2. **It is only necessary to outperform the market by a few percentage points to end up with vast amounts more wealth**. Once you have created the core of your snowball (some money plus sound principles), just keep adding steadily through good returns over the medium term, and keep it moving in a downhill direction by not deviating from those principles.

3. **It's only investing if you have made a thorough analysis of the company, there is a built-in margin of safety and the objective is set as merely a satisfactory return.** If any of these characteristics are missing then you are speculating.

4. **Do not accept Mr Market's valuation of a share; do your own research.** Mr Market is a manic depressive, sometimes valuing the same company in the same circumstance highly and then, in short order, seeing only the negatives and therefore willing to sell it cheaply. Exploit market irrationality rather than participating in it.

PART 2.
INVESTMENT DEALS

Investment 1

CITIES SERVICES

Summary of the deal

Deal	Cities Services
Time	1941, Buffett aged 11
Price paid	$38.25 per share
Quantity	3 shares
Sale price	$40 per share
Profit	$5.25

At the heart of Warren Buffett's investment philosophy is clarity on what makes someone an investor as opposed to a speculator. It is surprising how many players in the financial markets fail to get to grips with this.

Clear thinking on this point is needed to set the share buyer on a path with less risk and fewer mistakes, resulting in long-term wealth building – the get rich slowly approach. I'll begin to explain the Buffett philosophy by tracing the influences on him from an early age. Recalling the way he built up his portfolio from virtually nothing is an inspiration in itself.

Childhood

Buffett was born in August 1930, shortly after the Wall Street Crash of 1929 and therefore at the beginning of the Great Depression. His father was a stockbroker in Omaha, Nebraska, who became, for a time, a congressman. So the family were not particularly wealthy, but they were able to weather the Depression in reasonable shape, much helped by typical Midwestern family unity. However, it was all too plain to a bright young Buffett what destitution looks like – it was all around. He was determined to become wealthy.

As a youngster he tried all sorts of ways of making a dollar. He would collect lost golf balls (or even better, get a friend to collect them) and sell them. He would buy packs of Coca-Cola, break them up and sell them individually. He bought an old Rolls-Royce and hired it out.

Pinball machines in barbershops were a favourite – Buffett would buy the machines, set them up in the barbershop and the barber would get a share of the takings. The biggest money-spinner was the delivery of *Washington Post* newspapers; when the family moved to Washington for a while he would get up early to fulfil his duties on three newspaper routes before school.

By being so active, Buffett managed to save a few thousand dollars by his mid-teenage years. At the age of 15 he was able to invest $1,200 to buy a 42-acre farm, 70 miles from Omaha, from which he got a share of the profits (the land was sold at double the price five years later).

First shares

As early as 11 years old, Buffett had $120 of savings – representing six years of graft and scrimping up to that point. He combined this with his sister Doris's money and bought six shares in Cities Services Preferred – his three shares cost $114.75.

By June the shares had fallen from $38.25 to $27. Buffett felt guilty because he had persuaded his sister to trust him and buy the shares with her savings. This sense of responsibility to those who trust him is very important in understanding the way Buffett went on to treat partners in the 1950s and 1960s, and then shareholders in Berkshire Hathaway.

Fortunately the shares recovered to $40, at which point Buffett sold. This realised a profit of $1.75 per share.

College

Aged 17, Buffett went to the Wharton School at the University of Pennsylvania. After a short time he became unsure of continuing his studies, asking himself what the point of it was. He had been in business since he was six, already had a good income, and college would slow his progress. He believed he knew more than the professors about how to run a business.

He got through the classes easily and managed to stick it for two years, while pursuing other interests, but did not finish the course at Wharton. He switched to the University of Nebraska, closer to his family.

Following stocks – as a speculator

Instead of prioritising college work, Buffett was obsessed, as always, with money making. At this time he supervised paperboys in six Nebraska counties, collected golf balls and worked as a salesman at J. C. Penney.

By 1949 his savings amounted to around $9,800. He was hooked on share trading at this time. He tried all sorts of ways to make share trading work, from chart patterns to numerical patterns and 'odd-lot stock trading', whatever that was. We can tell from this that Buffett had been speculating.

And then he read Benjamin Graham's new book *The Intelligent Investor* in 1949. It was a revelation! Buffett was now desperate to go to Colombia Business School to study the course designed and presented by Graham and David Dodd. This he did in the fall of 1950, graduating with a Master of Science in Economics in the summer of 1951. Within that degree programme he could really focus his attention on the course devised by these founding fathers of value investing. Buffett lapped up Graham and Dodd's rational approach to share selection.

Learning points

1. **Do not unthinkingly grab at a small profit**. Cities Services Preferred soared to $202 after Buffett had sold for $40.

2. **Do not fixate on what you paid for a share**. That is a sunk cost. What is of interest is your estimation of where the price will go from here. If a share falls after purchase you must evaluate its prospects from this point, given your estimation of intrinsic value. In many cases intrinsic value does not rise and fall in tandem with the price.

3. **When investing other people's money, ill feeling can be created if a mistake is made.** Buffett hated confrontation and bad feeling so he swore that he would not take other people's money unless he was convinced he could succeed. John Templeton, a billionaire investor with strong Christian beliefs, used to say "OPM is sacred"; OPM being other people's money.

Investment 2

GEICO

Summary of the deal

Deal	GEICO
Time	1951, Buffett aged 20
Price paid	$10,282
Quantity	350 shares
Sale price	$15,259
Profit	$4,977

This example shows an early application of Graham's methods by Buffett.

The 20-year-old Buffett was into his second (and final) term at Columbia. By this point he had read *Security Analysis* many times, committing the case studies to memory. He entered Graham's classes in the spring term fully armed with Graham and Dodd's ideas; and he wanted to talk about them. He was first in the class to put his hand up and the most eager to engage Graham in discussion on the merits of a company, or comparison of a pair of companies (Graham's preferred teaching method). Later in the year Buffett received an A+ from Graham – the only one he ever gave.

Early in 1951, Buffett noticed that Graham was the chairman of a small insurance firm, Government Employees Insurance Company (GEICO). He was intrigued and wanted to know much more. On a Saturday he caught the train to Washington DC and knocked on the door of GEICO's headquarters. Before I go further, I'd better explain how GEICO came to be controlled by Graham's fund, the Graham-Newman Corporation.

GEICO history

GEICO was started in 1936 to provide motor insurance for government workers. It had chosen an unusual distribution technique. Most of its competitors sold insurance through brokers, but GEICO thought this expensive and realised it could offer better rates and gain higher profit margins if it sold insurance directly to people via mail order. It thrived, but in 1947 one of the controlling families wanted to sell their shares, which represented 55% of the company. They hired an investment broker, Lorimer Davidson, to handle the sale. At first he struggled but eventually, in 1948, Graham's fund bought the shares for $720,000 and Graham himself became chairman, with a directorship taken by one of his colleagues.

Buffett knocked at the door – on a Saturday!

On that Saturday in early 1951, the janitor opened the door of GEICO HQ and said that, by chance, Lorimer Davidson was in the building (Davidson had been hired by the company as Financial Vice-President). When Buffett explained he was a student of Graham's, and he quickly demonstrated in conversation that he had read up about the firm, and asked pertinent questions, Davidson became amenable to sacrificing a few minutes of his time to chat with the young man (by Buffett's own admission, he looked like a 16-year-old geek at this time).

Four hours later they emerged and Buffett had been given a wonderful lesson in the workings of an insurance company. He could see clearly that GEICO had two competitive advantages:

1. A very low-cost distribution method.

2. A good, niche market. Customers who, almost by definition, were safe drivers and therefore a low insurance risk, were in the habit of buying insurance from GEICO.

Growth prospects were excellent, not least because GEICO had a very efficient sales team. Profit margins were five times those of the average insurer. Even better, it had a substantial cash float (insurance premiums paid but not claimed on), leaving this cash available for investment purposes.

Thus we see an early example of Buffett undertaking deep analysis on a business, trying to establish in his mind its intrinsic value. We also see Buffett sticking to his opinion rather than following that of experts; he had spoken to a few insurance investment specialists who said that GEICO was overvalued. GEICO only had a 1% market share and was thought to be vulnerable to aggressive competition, especially agent-based distribution systems. But Buffett had learned from Graham, who said you are neither right nor wrong because the crowd disagrees with you. Look to the facts, not the crowd.

Excitedly, Buffett invested about 65% of his net worth in GEICO stock for the sum of $10,282.

Buffett sold in 1952 for $15,259. Not a bad return, but consider this: if he had held on to those same shares and gone fishing for the next 19 years they could have been sold for $1.3m in the late 1960s. The painful lesson was in the *inadvisability of selling a stake in an identifiably wonderful company*. But, let's forgive him. As we will see, he put the money to good use elsewhere.

It is worth noting that Berkshire Hathaway invested in GEICO again in the early 1970s. In 2016, GEICO had 11.4% of the US auto insurance market.

Learning points

1. **Do your homework.** When analysing a business look at the quantitative factors, such as the accounts, and the qualitative factors, such as the reputation of the company with its customers or the talent of its management.

2. **It is possible for you to see much more than the so-called experts if you are prepared to make some effort.** In this instance, many analysts at the major fund houses never bothered to visit and talk to managers at small insurance firms, preferring to look at annual reports and industry reports only. All investors can apply this lesson – by going one step further you can become more knowledgeable than professionals.

3. **Look for businesses that make profitable use of capital.** If a business is using ploughed-back capital to generate superior rates of return on its operations, this can be highly valuable. In such circumstances profits are likely to rise rapidly, followed by the share price.

Investments 3 and 4

CLEVELAND WORSTED MILLS AND A GAS STATION

On graduation from Columbia with his A+, Buffett was very keen to work for Graham's company. Graham kept rejecting him – Graham was Jewish and there was much prejudice on Wall Street at the time, so he reserved jobs for Jews. Buffett even offered to work for nothing. He was still rejected. Buffett wryly noted that Graham took this value thing very seriously!

Somewhat reluctantly, the 21- year-old Buffett returned to Omaha to work as a stockbroker in his father's firm, living in his parents' house. As a broker he was supposed to push share transactions by actively coming up with ideas and trying to interest private investors in putting purchases through his father's brokerage.

Looking like a 16-year-old 'dork' he was not taken seriously when he asked the wealthy men and women of Omaha to buy his picks. The people he approached would sometimes listen, but would then consult a more mature stockbroker about the idea and end up trading through them. Or they'd ask, "What does your Dad think?". Despite the high quality of his ideas, Buffett was frustrated.

Investing

By the end of 1951, Buffett had boosted his capital to around $20,000. Both Graham and his father, the two men he most admired in the world, advised him not to invest in the stock market as prices were too high. He did not agree with their logic and made up his own mind, deciding that 1951 was a perfect time to pick up good companies. He thought the potential was so great that for the first time he borrowed money to buy shares (he borrowed a quarter of his net worth, $5,000).

Be warned, borrowing is for very able investors and those than can afford to lose the entire portfolio without affecting their lifestyle. I do not advise it for others and nor does Buffett. In fact, Buffett did very little borrowing thereafter (his insurance float gave him the leverage he needed, usually for free).

With his capital of $25,000 and in search of investments, Buffett went through the Moody's manual summaries of all American listed firms – some 10,000 pages – twice. Some he rejected within seconds, others he learned about inside-out. He also emulated Graham by teaching Graham's methods and his own ideas at an investment night class at the University of Omaha. Around this time, Buffett had two failed investment deals.

Failure 1: Cleveland Worsted Mills

Cleveland Worsted Mills had a share price of less than half the business' net current asset value (NCAV). This meant that the total price of all the company's shares (the market capitalisation) was less than half of the amount of money tied up in the business' current assets after deduction of all liabilities. In practice, if the company paid off all its creditors and the fixed assets were worth nothing, it would still have money in the form of cash, receivables (debtors) and/or inventories worth double the price that the market was currently offering for its shares. This method of share selection is so important to the Buffett story in the 1950s that I explain it in more detail below.

As well as Cleveland Worsted Mills selling at half its NCAV, it paid a high proportion of its earnings in dividends. These combined factors made Cleveland appear an attractive investment and Buffett sold the idea of this investment to stockbroker clients in Omaha. Then it went wrong – the company faced intense competition from textile plants in the southern US states and from synthetic fibres. It made large losses, cut its dividend and its share price dropped.

As mentioned above, net current asset value investing is so important to Buffett's approach that it is worth me taking a moment to expand on this subject in more detail.

Net current asset value investing

Believe it or not, hidden in the depths of the stock market are companies that sell for less than the value of their current assets. Current assets are cash and other assets that are expected to be converted to cash within a year. They consist mostly of inventories, receivables and cash.

More remarkable still is the fact that if you deduct all liabilities, both long- and short-term, from these current assets – to produce a net current asset value – you can find companies that sell for less than this net current asset value (NCAV).

This is even more astonishing if we consider that this approach ignores the value of the long-term assets (otherwise referred to as non-current assets or fixed assets) held by the business. These assets are valued at zero. This is conservative valuation taken to an extreme. It may be that the long-term assets are comprised of buildings, vehicles, plant, etc., with a significant market value. And yet all of that is ignored – it is counted at zilch.

There are then two more layers of caution applied on top of that:

1. Reduce inventories and receivables

The figures for the valuation of current assets in the business' balance sheet are not taken at face value. It could be that you want to build in a margin of safety to your valuation of inventories. For example, managers, through their accountants, will have stated a particular figure at the accounting date for the value of raw materials in the warehouse, for half-finished goods on the production line and for completed products not yet sold to customers. But it is not unheard of for managers to view things through rose-tinted spectacles. As value investors we can build in a margin of safety by refusing to value on the basis of the best possible outcome. Perhaps some of the old stock is now obsolete and could not be sold at anything like the original cost. As outsiders we cannot go through every item and value it, but we could, just to be on the safe side, reduce the overall inventories value by say 33%. This was the percentage reduction recommended by Benjamin Graham in most instances.

The same safety principle goes for receivables (otherwise referred to as debtors). The managers of the business may be more optimistic than you in guessing the proportion of customers who will not pay. Perhaps the receivables figure should be lowered by 20%.

2. Check the qualitative factors

The next step is to ensure that the qualitative characteristics of the company are sound (assuming that the best course of action for the business is not immediate liquidation):

(a) **Prospects for the business**. Is the operating business reasonably well positioned to offer profits over the medium to long term? Believe it or not, it is perfectly possible to find good businesses selling on low prices relative to the net current asset value. 'Earnings power', a term coined by Graham, is what we are looking for. Graham said that one indicator of future earnings power is a satisfactory level of current earnings and dividends, and/or high average earnings power in the past. Here, it is important not to rely on someone else's projections of great things to come, or on past data alone: this may be misleading. For example, in 2012, J. C. Penney, Nokia or Tesco looked strong based upon data or facts from the past. But as these companies found, the competitive environment can change. The investor must scan beyond the data for signs of vulnerability to disruption to business as usual.

Earnings power is not the current earnings, but is derived from a combination of actual earnings over a period of five to ten years and estimated future earnings over, say, five years in the future. This takes into account the competitive strengths of the business vis-à-vis rivals, suppliers and customers, as well as the potential for new rivals to enter the industry and for substitute products/services to damage the firm (for example, in the way that the internet has provided a substitute for travel agents, recorded music distribution and book selling).

(b) **Quality of management**. There are two aspects to consider here:

1. *Competence*: Statements by management are examined and compared with their performance over a long period.

2. *Shareholder orientation*: If a business has competent and energetic management it still may not be a good investment unless that management also possesses the quality of integrity, particularly with regard to serving shareholder interests.

(c) **Stability.** Is the operating business reasonably stable? Will the debt level carried by the firm significantly hurt its stability prospects? The investor does not want to be invested in a company with high levels of borrowing or highly variable income flows. Industries that are not subject to much change are likely to be stable; this means bio-tech and computer game software would be out, whereas industries such as selling boring widgets are more likely to be in.

What leads to such lowly priced shares?

There are three reasons that even companies with large surpluses of current assets over liabilities see their share prices fall to below NCAV:

1. The managers have pursued value-destroying activities that have whittled away shareholder's assets through losses year after year.

2. The stock market has irrationally pushed the price of the shares down to unreasonable levels.

3. Shareholders have not pressed the company to do the right thing by shareholders.

Why should a share with high net current asset value rise?

Companies going through a torrid time, a few years of loss-making, or suffering from an economic or industry decline, are usually subject to a great deal of market pessimism. Sometimes this is indiscriminate. Alongside the dumping of dross, there is dumping of sound companies, where there are good grounds for believing that recovery will eventually occur.

There are four possible paths of development that might halt or reverse the pattern of losses, putting a stop to the destruction of value through the gradual dissipation of assets from the balance sheet year after year:

1. Earning power is lifted through an improvement in the economic background

This might be the result of a general economic recovery. Alternatively, earning power can also be lifted through the effects of exit from the industry: competitors go to the wall or withdraw from some activities, allowing the few left standing to increase prices and raise profits.

2. Management stir themselves

Management may be competent, but faced with a fierce onslaught from new competitors or aggressive pricing and marketing by old competitors. Perhaps they will regroup, learn from past mistakes and attack with renewed vigour.

3. A sale of the company to another

The buyer should be willing to pay the liquidating value at least (which, if current assets sell for close to their balance sheet values, will be higher than the pertaining market capitalisation), and so the NCAV investor gets a boost.

4. Complete or part liquidation

There are many companies where it simply does not make any sense to continue in existence. Far more money would be available for the shareholders if the directors chose to run down the assets by selling them off for cash. Then an increased stream of dividends could be paid to shareholders. With some companies, especially those holding a lot of property assets but making nothing but losses, two or three times as much money will flow to shareholders if a gradual liquidation of assets is implemented.

Thus, the NCAV investor is looking for one of these four events to earn a return on her investment.

Failure 2: The Gas Station

Buffett bought an Omaha gasoline station in partnership with a friend. Unfortunately, it was sited opposite a Texaco station that consistently outsold them. Amazingly, Buffett even took up physical work to help out – at weekends he actually served customers.

He learned lessons in competitive advantage: the Texaco station "was very well established and very well liked... customer loyalty... a clientele... Nothing we could do to change that." With this lesson absorbed, later it led to some of his best buys as he sought companies with the most pronounced customer loyalties in their industries, e.g. Coca-Cola.

But, at the time, the 22-year-old was smarting from losing $2,000 on petrol.

Sending ideas to Graham

Buffett still hankered after a resumption of his education under Graham's tutelage and so continued to send Graham analyses of companies. Eventually Graham and his partner, Jerry Newman, relented and offered Buffett a job at Graham-Newman Corporation. He was to be one of only four people, other than the partners, to work with them in their New York investment office.

Learning points

1. **Every investor will make mistakes – many of them**. You have to accept that you will have failures, this goes with the territory. You must develop personality traits that allow you to put failure into perspective: the overall portfolio performance over the long run is your focus for judging success/failure. Even great investors will get it wrong 45% of the time. If you are right 55% of the time, over a span of years you will have a wonderful increase in wealth.

2. **NCAV investing was central to Buffett's approach**. It's possible for share prices to fall so low that the current assets per share within the company after deducting all the liabilities become worth significantly more than the price at which the market is offering the shares. Some of these companies have good odds of recovery of shareholder value.

3. **Do not neglect the qualitative factors**. Understanding the competitive position and quality of management are central to most successful investments.

Investment 5

ROCKWOOD & CO.

Summary of the deal

Deal	Rockwood & Co.
Time	1954–55, Buffett aged 23–24
Price paid	various
Quantity	N/A
Sale price	various
Profit	$13,000

Working for Graham, Buffett had two years of intense activity. His main job was to plough through data on hundreds of companies in a windowless room. He prepared simple reports on companies that fitted Graham's criteria, in particular net current asset value shares. They were cheap, neglected, unloved shares.

This investment is an example of one of Buffett's brilliant investments in a grossly undervalued company, which was overlooked by others because it failed to make a profit.

Rockwood and Co.

A chocolate bits maker (for chip cookies) with a history of losses, Rockwood had a large inventory of cocoa beans. Furthermore, cocoa bean prices were high. If Rockwood sold the beans on the market it would incur a large tax bill. As an alternative, the directors of Rockwood asked Graham-Newman Corporation if they would like to buy the company. But, the asking price was too high.

Then Rockwood asked another able investor, Jay Pritzker, if he would like to buy the company. Pritzker thought of a way to avoid the 50% tax bill on the profits from selling the beans. A new tax regulation said that if a business was reducing its scope, it could avoid tax on a partial liquidation of its inventory. Pritzker bought a controlling stake and started to liquidate the $13m of cocoa beans. But he did not sell them for cash. He said that shareholders in Rockwood could exchange each of their shares for $36 of beans. The shares were selling on the market at $34. Thus, a clear arbitrage opportunity arose. Graham was awake to this and Buffett was instructed to buy shares in Rockwood in order to exchange them for cocoa beans, and then to sell the beans, resulting in a profit of $2 per share each time.

Rather than a bag of beans, what Rockwood actually gave each seller was a warehouse certificate showing ownership of the beans. In case the price of the certificates fell, Graham-Newman Corporation sold cocoa futures (guaranteeing to deliver a fixed quantity of beans at a future date for a fixed price), thus locking-in their arbitrage profit. Week after week Buffett had to buy shares, then sell bean futures.

The Buffett twist

Graham-Newman was doing very well out of the arbitrage trade, but Buffett believed he could do even better. He simply went out and bought 222 shares in Rockwood. His logic was as follows:

- The offer was 80lbs of beans per share.

- The beans Rockwood owned amounted to significantly more than 80lbs per outstanding share.

- So if you were one of the shareholders who did NOT sell your shares to Rockwood, first your quantity of beans per share held by the company was larger than the $36 on offer; and second, your quantity of beans per share grew as others sold their shares.

- In addition to the beans was the value of all the company's plant, machinery, equipment, cash, receivables, etc., held within the profitable rump of the business, which was being retained.

Pritzker knew all this and was a very smart cookie. Buffett aligned his interests with Pritzker's by buying shares.

What was the outcome?

Before Pritzker's offer, shares in Rockwood sold for $15. They went up to around $100. Buffett made a profit of $13,000.

Learning points

1. **It is important to thoroughly consider a company's actions and their impact on future value** (as opposed to thinking of things as a short-term, virtually risk-free payback).

2. **These opportunities only come along to those willing to do the groundwork** day after day, looking for that needle in a haystack. Buffett examined thousands of companies, hoping to find one or two more goldmines like Rockwood.

Investment 6

SANBORN MAPS

Summary of the deal

Deal	Sanborn Maps
Time	1958–60, Buffett aged 28–30
Price paid	About $45, roughly $1m
Quantity	24,000 shares or 22.8% of the company's shares
Sale price	Sanborn shares exchanged for a portfolio of shares
Profit	Roughly 50%

Graham retired when Buffett had worked for him for two years and Buffett was made unemployed. By this time in 1956, Buffett had accumulated around $140,000–$174,000 (which varies depending on which source you consult) and he was not looking for a job. He just wanted a sound base from which to think and make investment decisions about American companies. He chose Omaha.

On returning to Omaha, the 25-year-old Buffett decided to concentrate on investment for himself. He also set up a small investment partnership with six sleeping partners – mostly relatives and local friends, such as his aunt Alice who chipped in $35,000. The partnership raised $105,000, with Buffett putting in only $100. He worked in a small room off his bedroom.

Buffett was the sole decision-maker and he did not tell the partners what he was investing in (for fear of copycats). However, he did provide an annual report on overall performance and his wife Susie put on a chicken dinner for the annual gathering. It was not long before other investors were attracted (some were former investors of Ben Graham's looking for a new home for their money), and Buffett consented to establish more partnerships, all consolidated into the single BPL in 1962.

Buffett Partnership fee structure and performance

Buffett felt it was wrong to take a fee from his partners unless he could at least match the return they could get by safely lending out their money. Thus, he said that he would not charge a fee for a given year unless he gained 4% in that year for the partners (this was for the period 1956–61). However, any return above 4% would result in a high proportion going to Buffett. This performance fee was initially up to 50%; from 1961 the hurdle was 6% and the performance fee 25% on returns above that.

Buffett set himself the aim of outperforming the Dow over any three-year period – three years being the minimum period of time over which he thought a fund manager should be judged. Table 6.1 shows the performance of the Buffett partnerships from 1957–1968 – this is the longest period for which we have sound data before the consolidated Partnership was liquidated in early 1970.

Table 6.1: Performance of the Buffett partnerships (1957–68)

Year	Dow return (%)	Partnership return (%)	Limited partners' results (after fees to Buffett) (%)
1957	-8.4	+10.4	+9.3
1958	+38.5	+40.9	+32.2
1959	+20.0	+25.9	+20.9
1960	-6.2	+22.8	+18.6
1961	+22.4	+45.9	+35.9
1962	-7.6	+13.9	+11.9
1963	+20.6	+38.7	+30.5
1964	+18.7	+27.8	+22.3
1965	+14.2	+47.2	+36.9
1966	-15.6	+20.4	+16.8
1967	+19.0	+35.9	+28.4
1968	+7.7	+58.8	+45.6
Compound 1957–68	+185.7	+2610.6	+1403.5
Average annual rate	9.1	31.7	25.3

Source: BPL letter to partners (22 January 1969)

In this period from 1957 to 1968, Buffett did not have a down year. He obtained treble the Dow annual return on average (before deducting his fee).

Once the partnership capital accumulated to a few million dollars, Buffett took a very large annual fee for himself, which he put back into the partnerships, building up his share, and becoming rich.

Here is an example of one of the deals Buffett made in this period.

Sanborn Maps

Sanborn Maps was a company down on its luck. It had once been a thriving business providing maps to insurance companies. The maps displayed minute detail on power lines, water mains and buildings for every US city, to allow estimation of fire risk. As insurance companies merged they bought fewer copies of Sanborn's detailed street plans. Also, modern methods of assessing and mitigating risk were introduced.

Despite this, Sanborn still had a sales volume of around $2m a year and remained profitable, although profits had reduced from over $500,000 per year in the late 1930s to under $100,000 in 1958 and 1959. The share price dropped as profits fell, from $110 in 1938 all the way to $45 in 1958. This made the market capitalisation of the company $4.7m ($45 x 105,000 shares).

Significantly, in addition to the map business, Sanborn had an investment portfolio that amounted to $65 a share – that is, it had around $7m of marketable securities producing a sizable income.

The directors, who owned very few shares, had been content for the company to simply hold the portfolio and collect their salaries. They even had the nerve to cut the dividend five times over the previous eight years, despite the massive quantity of liquid resources within the firm.

Buffett bought, but needed control to effect change

We can get an insight into Buffett's thoughts about Sanborn from this extract from a letter he wrote to partners in 1959:

"In effect, this company [Sanborn Maps] is partially an investment trust owning some thirty or forty other securities of high quality. Our investment was made and is carried at a substantial discount from asset value based on market value of their securities and a conservative appraisal of the operating business."[4]

Buffett bought Sanborn's shares for his partnerships, starting in November 1958 and throughout 1959. He also bought Sanborn shares for his personal fund and encouraged friends to buy stakes. He wanted as many people with loyalty to him as possible to own its shares because he needed to gain voting power to push for the changes required to release the value in the company. Sure enough, through his partnerships, personal account, and friends and family, Buffett managed to buy enough shares to achieve his election to the board. The rest of the directors were mostly insurance company representatives – Sanborn's largest customers.

At his first board meeting, Buffett proposed that shareholders receive the value in the company's investment portfolio and that Sanborn should re-establish the earning power of its map business by making the data more user-friendly through electronic devices. The insurance directors said no, but the other directors were in favour.

Buffett was angry that the insurance director board members had sought to block his ideas, so his partnerships and his coterie of friends and family kept buying shares (he even roped in his father to persuade his brokerage clients to invest). This gave Buffett enough of a stake to take control of the company should he want to. His partnership had 24,000 shares, or 22.8% of Sanborn, and his *associates* had another 21% or so. Buffett had put 35% of his partners' money into Sanborn Maps. Further insight into Buffett's thinking can be found in this extract from a letter to partners in 1958:

> "While the degree of undervaluation is no greater than in many other securities we own… we are the largest stockholder and this has substantial advantages many times in determining the length of time required to correct the undervaluation. In this particular holding we are virtually

assured of a performance better than that of the Dow-Jones for the period we hold it."[5]

Buffett used this power to tell the other Sanborn directors that if they did not do as he suggested, he would call a special shareholders' meeting and take directorial control. In 1960 the board agreed to use the portfolio to buy out shareholders. Buffett's partnership tendered their shares. Buffett's partners made a profit of around 50%. As Buffett described it:

> "About 72% of the *Sanborn* stock, involving 50% of the 1,600 stockholders, was exchanged for portfolio securities at fair value. The map business was left with over $1.25 million in government and municipal bonds as a reserve fund… The remaining stockholders were left with a slightly improved asset value, substantially higher earnings per share, and an increased dividend rate."[6]

Learning points

1. **Margin of safety**. Clearly Buffett made good use of Graham's ideas here. He bought the shares with a decent margin of safety at less than net current asset value. And he had the reassurance that there was some earning power, which would improve further if the business was modified or downsized – indeed, it still operates today. An additional reassurance came with controlling so many shares because of the influence he could have on the direction of the firm.

2. **Greater clout when you marshal millions**. The advantage of working with larger sums of money is that it allows the investor to gain control of a business. And, as the access to funds grows, the investor can target companies where current control is less likely to be in the hands of a small dominating director group. Thus we see a 29-year-old Buffett working with others to maximise shareholder value against the will of an apparently entrenched board. This required significant drive

and a sense of purpose he could communicate to persuade others in his *concert party* (or collection of independent concerned shareholders, depending on how you look at it). Despite Buffett's instinct to recoil from confrontation, when it came to shareholder value he could be seriously combative.

Investment 7

DEMPSTER MILL

Summary of the deal

Deal	Dempster Mill
Time	1956–63, Buffett aged 26–32
Price paid	$28
Quantity	About 35,700 or 70% of the company's shares
Sale price	$80
Profit	$2.3m or 230%

The BPL, formed from the individual partnerships on 1 January 1962, started with $7.2m of net assets. Buffett put almost all of his own money into the partnership, which was slightly less than $450,000. In addition, he had a share of the value of the partnership because of the fees he had charged and ploughed back into it.

Dempster Mill

Dempster Mill was a small, family-owned business based in the Nebraska town of Beatrice. It supplied windmills and irrigation systems. Buffett began acquiring a few shares in 1956 when they were selling at $16–$18. It had a net worth (book value) of about $4.5 million, or $75 per share. Net current asset value was about $50 per share and annual sales about $9m.

The share price was so low because Dempster kept making small profits or losses, and the management seemed clueless as to how to correct this miserable pattern. Also, it had a lot of debt and was in an industry with very poor economics. Buffett said of Dempster:

> "The operations for the past decade have been characterized by static sales, low inventory turnover and virtually no profits in relation to invested capital."[7]

It was, in short, a typical Benjamin Graham type of investment. There were various possibilities for creating a return on such an investment. First, the economics of the industry might improve; second, the management might improve or be replaced; third, the business might be liquidated; and fourth, a takeover bid might be accepted.

Buffett and his friends, Walter Schloss and Tom Knapp, accumulated 11% of the company's shares, and Buffett joined the board. He kept on buying, eventually purchasing the Dempster family stake. The Buffett Partnership became the majority shareholder in mid-1961, with 70% of the equity costing about $1m (with another 10% held by a few associates), and Buffett was appointed chairman. The average price paid was $28 per share. The Dempster holding represented 21% of BPL's assets.

Trouble at Mill

The company engaged in a lot of unprofitable business ventures, using large amounts of shareholders' money in inventory and receivables. The logical thing to do was to cut drastically, releasing cash for deployment elsewhere, especially the purchase of other stock market quoted value shares. The managers nodded when

Chairman Buffett spoke about reducing inventory on his monthly visits from Omaha – and then promptly did nothing.

The cash shortage was so worrying that Dempster's bankers considered closing the company down and in 1962 it was months away from disaster. Buffett faced the prospect of explaining to his partners that 21% of their assets had disappeared. It was looking like it was going to be a failure that reflected badly on his investment decision-making. However, from unpromising material Buffett was able to create a valuable business out of Dempster Mill – with a little help from his friends.

Charlie Munger

In 1959, Buffett met Charlie Munger. A fellow intellectual and Omahan (but by then in California), Munger was one of the few people who could keep up with Buffett and give as good as he got in well-considered discussion. They got on like a house on fire.

Munger had been a lawyer, to which Buffett said that the legal profession was fine as a hobby, but he could do better as an investor. Munger then started an investment fund in California and spoke on the phone regularly to Buffett about investment ideas. They discussed the problem of Dempster in spring 1962. Munger knew a tough-minded manager in California, Harry Bottle, who might be able to help. It took a generous pay package (mostly a profit share), but Buffett was able to persuade Bottle to move to Beatrice and it was worth it.

The restoration

Bottle went to Beatrice in April 1962, identified the loss-making areas of Dempster Mill and sacked people: it was not easy, but necessary. A newly hired employee of Buffett's, Bill Scott, went over to Beatrice to help Bottle sort through the inventory. Scott was formerly a banker and attendee of Buffett's investment course.

The only other employee Buffett had was a secretary in his tiny new office at Kiewit Plaza, Omaha.

Bottle and Scott revamped Dempster's marketing. They also sold surplus equipment, slashed inventory, closed five branches and raised prices for the rump business (for items where they were the sole suppliers, they increased prices by up to 500%). A proper cost data system was created. In all, 100 people were made redundant, despite union and local opposition. The breakeven point was virtually cut in half and released cash was invested by Buffett in shares and bonds.

Talking about the practical solutions he employed, Bottle said:

> "I was having trouble reducing inventories to a level that would accommodate a reasonable rate of return. So in desperation I simply hired a painter and with his help we painted a 6″ white line 10 feet above floor around the inside wall of our largest warehouse and I called in plant supervisors and informed them if I ever walked into the building and could not see the line above the pile of boxes I would lay off everyone, except the shipping department until the line was exposed. I gradually moved that line down until I arrived at a satisfactory inventory turn."[8]

Whereas inventory was $4.2m at the beginning of 1962, it was only about $1.6m one year later. On the other hand, whereas there was $166,000 of cash and $2,315,000 of liabilities at 30 November 1961 (Dempster's fiscal year end), this was transformed to about $1m in cash and investments (of the type bought by the Buffett Partnership) against total liabilities of $250,000. The share and bond portfolio rose to $2.3m in July 1963. Furthermore, Dempster now had a profitable operating business (worth at least $16 per share according to Buffett in his 1963 letter).

Realising the investment return

Buffett tried to sell the company, even running ads in the Wall Street Journal. The townsfolk of Beatrice were horrified at the prospect of another outsider roughing up their biggest employer, so they rallied round in the summer of 1963 and raised nearly $3m to buy the operating assets of the business as a going concern from the Dempster Mill Manufacturing Company. This left a shell, full of cash and investments, which was liquidated to pay shareholders cash, including the Buffett Partnership, which by then held 73% of the business. The partnership stake was now worth $3.3m, or $80 per share. Buffett had trebled the money he had put into Dempster Mill.

Learning points

1. **Business logic is one thing, being disliked is another, often overwhelming, thing**. A whole town disliked Buffett. He had a deep fear of confrontation and being loathed, and vowed never again to be in a situation where he had to be so brutal to the people who worked for him. This helps to explain much, for example the long period he continued the rubbish textile business in Berkshire Hathaway, his preference for sound franchise businesses with managers he likes, trusts and admires, who can grow a business over decades, and even his proclivity to hold shares through ups and down in a company's fortunes. Buffett likes building long-term positive relationships.

2. **Good managers can work wonders**. Buffett said, "Hiring Harry may have been the most important management decision I ever made. Dempster was in big trouble under two previous managers, and the banks were treating us as a potential bankrupt. If Dempster had gone down, my life and fortunes would have been a lot different from that time forward."[9]

3. **Patience will be rewarded**. There is no way to say this better than how Buffett said it himself: "It is to our advantage to have securities do nothing price-wise for months, or perhaps years, while we are buying them. This points to the need to measure our results over an adequate period of time. We suggest three years as minimum."[10]

4. **The importance of spotting companies using too much shareholders' money**. A company can be over-capitalised. Harry Bottle proved that Dempster had previously been using too much capital, because without raising any more money, by the summer of 1963 Dempster was employing only 60% of its assets in the manufacturing business. That was all that was needed for the productive elements of the business. The other 40% was available for Buffett to invest in marketable securities. Bottle discussed this in his letter of 20 July 1963 to Dempster stockholders: "This over-capitalisation presents important problems to the management in its efforts to produce a satisfactory return on the capital committed to the Corporation."

5. **The buying price is crucial**. If you buy at a low enough price then you have tilted the odds in your favour. As Buffett wrote, "Never count on making a good sale. Have the purchase price be so attractive that even a mediocre sale gives good results."[11]

6. **Look for pricing power**. There is hidden pricing power in many businesses. At Dempster, managers had previously not been bold enough to raise prices where they could. This ability to spot the potential for raising prices because of some degree of customer captivity was evident time and again in Buffett's career.

Investment 8

AMERICAN EXPRESS

Summary of the deal

Deal	American Express
Time	1964–68, Buffett aged 33–37
Price paid	Averaging around $71, totalling to $13m
Quantity	5% of the company's shares
Sale price	About $180 ($33m)
Profit	$20m or 154%

Warren Buffett always remembered the defining elements of an investment operation, as emphasised by Benjamin Graham:

- Thorough analysis of a business.

- Margin of safety.

- Expect only a satisfactory rate of return.

- Independence of mind, as expressed in the story of Mr Market, and the idea of intrinsic value were also important.

However, note that these principles can be applied in different value approaches. Graham emphasised high net current asset value situations, with a particularly keen eye on the margin of safety should the current business operations fail. But even he estimated earning power and stability, and considered managerial ability and integrity.

Buffett picked up many companies using this approach; we have already reviewed his investments in Rockwood, Sanborn Maps and Dempster Mill. Indeed, Buffett went on to select other shares based on this approach – including a certain Berkshire Hathaway.

A change of emphasis

By the early 1960s, Buffett found that many companies he analysed did not have particularly strong balance sheets and so would have been left to one side under Graham's approach. He found that in some instances these companies had good prospects because they had strong economic franchises combined with sound finances and able, honest managers.

This led to an evolution in Buffett's investment approach, which was assisted by the influence of the ideas of Philip Fisher[12] and regular conversations with Charlie Munger. This is not to say that Buffett rejected Graham's approach; merely that in the value orchard there are many types of ripe fruit.

One of the regular questions I've heard Buffett and Munger answer at their Omaha AGMs is: "What would you do if you were starting out with under $1m?" They reply that they would select much smaller companies where there are more opportunities to find undervaluation and where net asset values are high. They cannot deal with such small companies now that they have to invest billions to move the dial on their investment performance, and it is clear that buying and holding strong franchises for the long term is more rational when investing hundreds of millions.

Small investors can invest both ways: Graham-type value investments in small market capitalisation companies, as well as economic franchise shares – mostly larger companies. Larger investors do not have the option to invest in most net current asset value investments because they cannot invest meaningful amounts relative to the size of their fund without drastically moving the share price of the business they are buying.

An example of Buffett's modified investment method can be seen in his deal for American Express.

American Express

This story starts with a crook. He bought soybean-based salad oil and had it stored in warehouses. This oil had a daily price quoted in commodity markets and so the crook used his stock of oil as collateral to borrow from 51 banks.

American Express ran the warehouse housing the tanks and issued warehouse receipts confirming that the salad oil was there and could be traded. The banks were reassured and lent tens of millions of dollars to the crook.

You can see where this story is going, can't you? The clue to this simple scam is that oil floats on water, or that you can store salad oil in a small separate chamber positioned directly under the sampling hatch.

The crook realised he could borrow vast amounts more if American Express and the banks believed there was more salad oil in the tanks than there really was. He arranged for the tanks to be mostly filled with sea water and a layer of salad oil placed on top. When the inspectors from American Express or the banks trooped along they would take a sample from the top and would conclude that the tanks held large quantities of valuable oil.

The downfall

In September 1963, the crook grew very bold, thinking he could corner the market, which was especially attractive given the Soviet Union's need to import edible oils following crop failures. He borrowed from his broker on top of the loans he already had, to buy oil futures.

Then the US government prohibited the sale of oil to the Soviets and the price collapsed. The crook went bust in November and the banks lost over $150m. They turned to American Express to recoup their money and its share price plummeted from $64 to $38, as analysts worried about its survival.

Buffett's market research

In the early 1960s, American Express was the world leader in traveller's checks (it had 60% of the world market, even though it charged more than rivals), and the world leader in credit cards. Buffett went to one of his favourite diners in Omaha and watched. He found that ordinary people were still using their American Express cards when paying, total unfazed by the Wall Street salad oil scandal.

Buffett checked other restaurants and places where cards were used: merchants still accepted the cards. He went to banks and travel agencies and found that people still liked to use American Express traveller's cheques. He talked to American Express competitors and found that they thought it was still a serious rival. He contacted friends to see if people were still using cards and traveller's cheques outside of Omaha. Sure enough, they still valued the service and were unconcerned about the fuss on Wall Street.

Buffett concluded that the economic franchise was intact. It was a company with pricing power because it dominated its industry. It had customer captivity through its strong brand and network.

People still trusted the brand despite the slip up on salad oil. It had plenty of customer goodwill from its past reliability, which was a competitive advantage. Also, a huge cash float was created by people paying for traveller's cheques upfront. But, this was no *Grahamite* investment; American Express' balance sheet was too weak for that.

Buffett bought

In early 1964, the Buffett Partnership fund totalled $17m, of which Buffett owned $1.8m. He bought as many American Express shares as he dared without pushing up the price too much. By June 1964, the partnership held almost $3m of AmEx's shares.

As a shareholder, Buffett did not want American Express to shirk its responsibility for its part in the fraud because he knew that a company of this kind lives and dies by its reputation (a central component of its business franchise). It was better to take the financial hit now to preserve that reputation. Buffett thus endorsed the plan to settle with the banks for $60m. They did settle and the American Express share price rose quickly.

By November, the partnership had more than $4.3m in American Express stock and in early 1965 this holding accounted for almost one-third of the partnership's assets. Buffett kept buying. By 1966, the partnership had spent $13m on 5% of American Express's shares. In 1967 the share price rose to $180, at which point Buffett sold the bulk of the holding.

Learning points

1. **Think about the business**. There are times when short-term problems bring down a share price. In many situations the long-term value is unaffected. If the market concentrates only on the short term then the opportunity arises to buy excellent businesses with strong franchises and good managers on the cheap.

2. **When the odds are good, invest a lot**. Invest a meaningful amount of money if a brilliant opportunity comes along. Buffett put up to 40% of his fund in this one investment.

3. **Ask around for qualitative data**. Do your own scuttlebutt research (talking with anyone in the know) and don't rely on the opinion of analysts in their financial-centre tower blocks. A scuttlebutt on an old sailing ship was a barrel of drinking water. It became a place where the crew gathered to chat. Information was exchanged around the cask – or, in modern parlance, the water cooler – from rumour and opinion, to commentary and fact. Phillip Fisher used the term to mean going out to talk to anyone with a knowledge of a company. That might be competitors (e.g. asking, "Apart from yourselves, who is the best in the industry?"), employees, suppliers, customers, etc.

Investment 9

DISNEY

Summary of the deal

Deal	Disney
Time	1966–7, Buffett aged 35–6
Price paid	$4m
Quantity	5% of the company's shares
Sale price	$6.2m
Profit	$2.2m or 55%

In 1966, Disney's shares were selling at well under ten times the previous year's earnings per share. That is, Disney's shares were on a price-to-earnings ratio (PE) of less than 10.[13] Disney had earned around $21m profits before tax in 1965 and had a market capitalisation of between $80m and $90m. Furthermore, it had more cash than debt. The feeling on Wall Street was that despite its recent success with *Mary Poppins*, there was nothing in the pipeline, so little growth was in prospect – perhaps it would decline?

Buffett's actions

A key part of Buffett's research was to go and sit in the cinema surrounded by a whole bunch of children watching *Mary Poppins*. He could see how much they loved the Disney product for himself. And he could see that with the valuable back catalogue, people would keep paying for Disney films, generation after generation. The wonderful thing about *Snow White*, for example, is that once it has been made and you have written off the cost, you can bring it out again and again. Every seven years there is another cohort of youngsters keen to watch it. Furthermore, you can use the love of the characters in many different forms, from licensing on children's school bags and t-shirts to theme parks. And Mickey Mouse does not have an agent (unlike Tom Cruise, say), who might take much of the value generated by a film franchise for their client.

Buffett and Munger also visited Disneyland in California and walked around analysing the value of the rides. Buffett met Walt Disney and admired his devotion to his work and his infectious enthusiasm. Disney showed Buffett a ride that was being installed called *Pirates of the Caribbean*. This one ride alone cost $17m – about one-fifth of the company's market capitalisation. Buffett later quipped, "Imagine my excitement – a company selling at only five times rides!"[14]

The Buffett logic – more Fisher and Munger than Graham

Buffett was putting a great deal of weight on the intangible assets of Disney and paying little attention to the balance sheet assets. The film library alone was worth the purchase price, even though these assets never went near the balance sheet – the films were valued at zero! Buffett described his thought process as follows:

> "In 1966 people said, 'Well, *Mary Poppins* is terrific this year, but they're not going to have another *Mary Poppins*

next year, so the earnings will be down.' I don't care if the earnings are down like that. You know you've still got *Mary Poppins* to throw out in seven more years... I mean there's no better system than to have something where, essentially, you get a new crop every seven years and you get to charge more each time... I went out to see Walt Disney. We sat down and he told me the whole plan for the company – he couldn't have been a nicer guy. It was a joke. If he'd privately gone to some huge venture capitalist, or some major American corporation, if he'd been a private company, and said 'I want you to buy into this'... they would have bought in based on a valuation of $300 or $400 million dollars. The very fact that it was just sitting there in the market every day convinced [people that $80 million was an appropriate valuation]. Essentially, they ignored it because it was so familiar. But that happens periodically on Wall Street."[15]

Figure 9.1: Disney share price (1966–96)

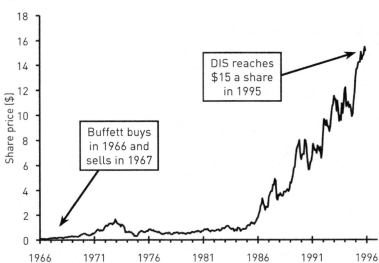

Source: Yahoo Finance

The Buffett Partnership bought 5% of the company for $4m. Buffett sold it the following year for $6.2m. Although this realised a nice profit, Buffett had sold too soon. Buffett said, "That decision [to buy in 1966] may appear brilliant... but your chairman was up to the task of nullifying it [by selling in 1967]."[16] He was referring to the fact that the share price rose 138-fold between 1967 and 1995.

Learning points

1. **Mr Market can be a Dumbo.** Not all the time, but sometimes. Look to the long term. Institutional investors can be focused on the short term. Try to out-think them by considering the position of the company once the current doldrums are over.

2. **Businesses needing little additional capital to generate increased profits can be a goldmine.** Disney has used the seven-year cycle to re-release old favourites to new generations of youngsters at little additional cost. And it has been able to use the film franchises in new formats as they have come along, from VHS to downloads, again at little additional cost of creation. Such businesses can produce very high returns on capital employed.

3. **Scuttlebutt again.** Buffett met with Walt Disney, and surveyed the company's brand and products at Disneyland and in cinemas.

4. **Observe quality in everyday life.** It's easy to see the quality of some companies' products or services just by keeping your eyes open.

5. **Don't sell too soon.** Buffett sold the Disney shares in 1967 for a 55% profit and kicked himself for doing so. There was more money on the table had he held on to the shares over the coming decades.

Investment 10

BERKSHIRE HATHAWAY

Summary of the deal

Deal	Berkshire Hathaway
Time	1962–present day
Price paid	$14.86 per share; total market capitalisation of BH $15m–$18m
Quantity	7% of the company's shares initially
Sale price	Trading today at $245,000 per share; market capitalisation over $400bn
Profit	Billions of dollars

In the 19th century, Hathaway Manufacturing Company was a thriving cotton spinning enterprise in New Bedford, Massachusetts. Profits soared when the military needed uniforms during the first world war. In the 1920s, cheap labour in the south took business away, and the Depression caused the closure of many mills in the New Bedford area. Owners took their money and invested it elsewhere.

But one firm was determined to stay in textiles: Hathaway. It had been run by Seabury Stanton since the end of the war. He had modernised by reinvesting $10m. Stanton and his brother, Otis, even borrowed personally to supply the business with investable capital.

Hathaway moved into artificial fibres such as rayon, becoming the dominant producer of linings for men's suits, and into fashion and curtains. But it lacked competitive advantage because it was unable to prevent new entrants to this market. Most frustrating was the entry of Far Eastern manufacturers with their lower costs. However, instead of withdrawing capital from the business, Seabury Stanton doggedly stuck to the textiles business as pressure mounted. Then, he doubled up by merging Hathaway with Berkshire Fine Spinning Associates in 1955.

Berkshire

Berkshire, another New England company, had been controlled by the Chace family for over 150 years. It made basic fabrics (for sheets, shirts, handkerchiefs, etc.). Malcolm Chace had run Berkshire since 1931, but by 1955 he had sadly concluded that additional investment in New England textiles was just throwing good money after bad.

Stanton, by contrast, remained confident of the power of his team's managerial prowess and felt safe with the combined balance sheet being so strong. He became president of the merged firm, while Malcolm Chace took up the role of chairman. The combined company had over 10,000 staff, 14 plants and annual sales of $112m. Stanton ordered new spindles and rebuilt looms.

However, Stanton's confidence was misplaced, and the difficulties increased still further in the next decade.

The decline after 1955

I was once with Warren Buffett and Charlie Munger, and the three of us were looking at Berkshire Hathaway's balance sheets from this period. Munger commented how small the balance sheet was back in the 1960s (when Buffett took control of the business). Buffett leaned over and took a look. He said, "That is the balance sheet for 1955!" and then pointed to another page saying, "That is the one for 1964 – it is much *smaller*!"

Table 10.1 shows a summarised Berkshire Hathaway balance sheet for 1955 that Munger said looked small when I showed it to him and Buffett.

Table 10.1: Berkshire Hathaway summarised balance sheet (September 1955)

Assets	
Cash	$4,169,000
Marketable securities	$4,580,000
Accounts receivable and inventories	$28,918,000
Net property, plant and equipment	$16,656,000
Other assets	$1,125,000
Liabilities	
Accounts payable and accrued expenses	-$4,048,000
Stockholders' equity (2,294,564 shares outstanding; book value $22.40 per share)	$51,400,000
Share price at beginning of 1955	About $14-$15
Market capitalisation	About $32m

In the nine years after 1955, sales aggregated to approximately $530m, but losses were made. The company more than halved its balance sheet over those nine years. This is shown in Table 10.2.

Table 10.2: Halving of Berkshire Hathaway equity (1955–64)

Stockholders' equity at September 30, 1955	$51,400,000
Additions to capital surplus	$888,000
Aggregate net loss from operations 1956–64	-$10,138,000
Cash dividends paid 1956–64	-$6,929,000
Repurchases of shares	-$13,082,000
Therefore stockholders' equity 3.10.64	$22,139,000

Operating losses accounted for some of the decline, but more important than that was the amount taken out by shareholders in dividends and share buy-backs. The business paid out $13m to buy slightly over one-half of its shares in this period. Table 10.3 shows the summarised balance sheet position in October 1964.

Table 10.3: Berkshire Hathaway summarised balance sheet (October 1964)

Assets	
Cash	$920,000
Accounts receivable and inventories	$19,140,000
Net property, plant and equipment	$7,571,000
Other assets	$256,000
Liabilities	
Accounts payable and accrued expenses	-$3,248,000
Debt: notes payable	-$2,500,000
Stockholders' equity (1,137,778 shares outstanding; book value $19.46 per share)	$22,139,000

Otis, Seabury Stanton's brother, did not agree with the strategy of reinvesting in textiles. This caused tension, as did the decision to promote Seabury's inexperienced son, Jack, to treasurer, with a view to him eventually becoming president. Both the Chace family and Otis judged Jack Stanton to be a poor choice and looked for an alternative.

Seabury's high-handedness was most devastating when he decided to break the implicit agreement with the New York Jewish families whose place in the value chain was to concentrate on finishing the fabric produced by his factories (dyeing and finishing). He set up his own finishing operations, competing with the families. The Jews of the finishing trade and the garment makers were not pleased, which led to reduced orders through New York, and the business declined another notch.

The economics of the industry were so bad by the late 1950s and early 1960s that even Seabury Stanton was in favour of closing unprofitable mills and releasing cash. Over the six years to 1961, half of the 14 plants were closed and the employee number dwindled to only 5,800. In 1962, Berkshire Hathaway lost $2.2m and the share price fell below $8 for a market capitalisation of under $13m.

Enter Warren Buffett and a "monumentally stupid" decision

In the mid-1950s, Benjamin Graham and his partner, Jerry Newman, looked closely at Berkshire Hathaway (BH). After all, its share price was close to net current asset value per share – an important criterion they sought in investments. Buffett watched the business from a distance following the 1955 merger, but it was not until the share price fell to $7.50 in December 1962 that he bought some of the company for BPL. At that time, BH had $10.25 of working capital per share and a book value of $20.20

(as stated in Buffett's 2014 letter to shareholders). Turnover was about $60m, but BH was down to just five mills.

Because BH continued to trade below its net current asset value level, Buffett bought more shares. At that time, he had no intention of taking over the company. The investment strategy was a typical Benjamin Graham *cigar butt* – it was so cheap that some hiccup in performance or a sale of shares to an enthusiastic buyer might allow an off-loading of the shares at a profit. As Buffett put it, "A cigar butt found on the street that has only one puff left in it may not offer much of a smoke, but the 'bargain purchase' will make the puff all profit."[17]

Seabury Stanton had got into the pattern of closing mills and thus releasing cash, followed by a share buy-back. Buffett's plan was to benefit from the next share buy-back. It was not long before two more plants were closed and more share repurchases were on the cards.

The fateful buy-back

Stanton decided to complete a buy-back in the spring of 1964. BH had 1,583,680 shares in issue, with the Buffett Partnership owning about 7%. Before publicly announcing the buy-back, Stanton spoke to Buffett and asked at what price the Buffett Partnership would sell. Buffett said $11.50; 50% above his purchase price. As Buffett said later, "There it was – my free puff, just waiting for me, after which I could look elsewhere for other discarded butts."[18]

"Fine, we have a deal," said Stanton. But a few days later on, 6 May 1964, Stanton sent a letter to all shareholders offering to buy 225,000 shares for *only* $11.375 – an eighth of a point less than he had agreed with Buffett.

Buffett said, "I bristled at Stanton's behaviour and didn't tender."[19] He could later see that this was a monumentally stupid decision – the industry economics were appalling and BH would in all probability continue to lose money. The sensible thing to do would have been to stick to Plan A and get a quick payoff. But instead, Buffett's irritation at Stanton's chiselling was such that instead of selling he actually *bought more shares* – aggressively. The average cost of the shares bought was $14.86. "Reflecting very heavy purchases in early 1965. The company on December 31, 1965 had net working capital alone of about $19 per share,"[20] Buffett later said of the situation.

Buffett's purchases included shares from Stanton's brother-in-law and from Malcolm Chace (the Chairman). By April 1965, Buffett had accumulated 392,633 out of 1,017,547 shares in issue. With that 38.6% he took control in a May board meeting (the market capitalisation at this time was about $18m).

It is amusing now to read how Buffett described what had happened: "Through Seabury's and my childish behaviour – after all, what was an eighth of a point to either of us? – he lost his job, and I found myself with more than 25% of BPL's capital invested in a terrible business about which I knew very little."[21]

Every penny of the $22m BH had was needed to run the textile business; it had no excess cash and was lumbered with $2.5m of debt. In a *Fortune* magazine article of 20 July 1998, Buffett said, "We went into a terrible business because it was cheap." He later said that the supposedly high working capital turned out to be a mirage. Berkshire was not only a cigar butt, but a soggy cigar butt at that. Talk about unpromising material with which to build a business empire!

Today, Berkshire Hathaway is one of the largest companies in the world (and many of the 1,200 shareholders of 1965 became millionaires within 20 years of Buffett taking control). How he got from there to here is a fascinating story with many useful lessons along the way. We'll start on the journey by illustrating the importance of Buffett finding the right leader, and placing a lot of trust in him.

The key person at Berkshire Hathaway in 1965 was not Buffett, but an up-from-the-ranks lifelong manufacturing manager. He was essential for Buffett to be able to cope with the firm, allowing him time to plan the needed transformation.

A visit to head office

As representative of the largest shareholder, Buffett was invited to look around the mill (this was before the May 1965 boardroom coup). Jack Stanton helped Buffett with some accounting data, but was too busy to show him around the plant. Big mistake!

Ken Chace (unrelated to Malcolm Chace of the Berkshire family) was asked to show Buffett around. An unpretentious 40-something manager, Chace had worked his way up to the position of chief of manufacturing. Otis Stanton and Malcolm Chace had already secretly earmarked Ken Chace as a candidate to take over as CEO.

Chace and Buffett talked, on and off, for two days. Buffett wanted to know about every aspect of the business, with a particular interest in solving the problem of low profitability. He wanted to know all the problems and the way in which Ken Chace would solve them. Chace's candour appealed to Buffett.

Ever since the Dempster Mill incident, Buffett knew a struggling business needed to be run by the right person for it to succeed. Could this person be trusted to be both competent and possess the quality of integrity with regard to shareholders' interests? Buffett concluded that modest Ken Chace was that man.

But Chace had other ideas

Ken Chace had already been looking for another job, as he was only too painfully aware that BH had little future. He had been talking to a competitor about joining them.

Stanley Rubin, who worked for BH as vice president for sales, knew Buffett and was aware, or guessed, that Buffett would soon take control of BH. He also surmised that Buffett wanted Ken Chace in charge afterwards. He telephoned Ken Chace in early 1965 and pleaded with him not to leave his post. In April 1965, Chace and Buffett met in New York for ten minutes. Buffett told Chace he wanted him to be president of BH. He explained that he had enough shares to get control of the company at the next director's meeting, but to keep this conversation quiet until then.

It was made plain that the operating business was to be Chace's baby; Buffett did not do regular management. Indeed, Buffett's role in the companies he controls is three-fold:

1. Capital allocation.

2. Selecting the key person(s) and thinking through the right incentive package.

3. Cheering on the managers who are performing well. He does not need regular meetings or briefings, but he does like to read the numbers coming from the operating units.

Buffett had already persuaded many of the Chace family of the old Berkshire (remember, not Ken Chace's family) to sell their shares to him. Otis Stanton also agreed to sell, on condition that Buffett made the same offer to his brother, Seabury. By spring 1965, BH was down to two mills and 2,300 employees. In the May board meeting Stanton resigned and stormed out with his son Jack. Ken Chace was elected president. Otis Stanton voted for the changes and stayed on the board. Within a couple of years, the Buffett Partnership had nearly 70% of BH's shares.

But what do you do with a small declining New England textile company filled with pessimistic employees? It was quite a conundrum.

Berkshire Hathaway: one boss, one president and a rubbish business

In 1965, Buffett had to concentrate on running the investment partnership from his Omaha base. Even though a significant proportion of his partners' money was invested in Berkshire Hathaway, he still had to analyse hundreds of other companies to select shares for the portfolio.

Buffett didn't have a clue how to run a textile business, but he did have a born and bred New Bedford man who had spent his entire adult life in the industry – Ken Chace – as president of the company. Warren Buffett, as *chairman of the executive committee*, was the real boss. (Malcolm Chace remained chairman.)

Then Buffett took BH through eight stages, or orders of business, to get it organised. These were as follows.

1. Get rid of the liquidator reputation

Buffett had been hurt greatly by the loathing the people of Beatrice developed for him when he closed down some of Dempster Mill's operations and made dozens unemployed.

He immediately spoke to the New Bedford press saying that the business would carry on as normal; there would be no mill closings. By a stroke of luck, BH happened to face an improving market for synthetic cloth at that time. It looked as though profits were going to come its way – and they did so for two years (only!).

2. Allocation of tasks

Buffett was true to his word: anything to do with the mill operations was up to Ken Chace. Buffett's job was to look after the money.

3. Incentives

Buffett does not like executive options because they offer rewards without the downside risk, and they encourage managers to gamble with shareholders' money. Instead, he offered Ken Chace the chance to buy 1,000 shares. He was earning only $30,000 per year and so could not fund the purchase. Buffett offered to lend the $18,000 he needed, and Chace accepted. Chace showed great faith in both himself as a manager, and his new boss, Buffett, who might do great things with this tiny company.

4. Focus on return on capital employed

Buffett explained to Ken Chace that he was not particularly focused on the level of output of the mills, nor on the volume of sales, nor market share. Also, looking at profit was an inadequate way of setting a target for the business.

The reason for this is that examination of the size of profit is insufficient if it is not considered alongside the amount of shareholders' money that has been devoted to achieving that profit. In other words, what really matters is the percentage return on capital employed. Ken Chace was to be judged using this metric.

Buffett said of this, "I'd rather have a $10m business making 15% than a $100m business making 5%. I have other places I can put the money."[22]

5. Release cash

Buffett made it plain that existing cash was not being used to generate adequate returns in BH. Chace was tasked with releasing cash as much as he could. Related to this, he was asked to produce monthly financial reports.

6. Send bad news early

Chace was asked to warn Buffett if unpleasant surprises might be around the corner.

7. Praise key people

People respond to signals that they are appreciated; it's only fair that they are told they are doing a good job if that is the case. Buffett never forgot to commend his managers for performing well. In the partnership's 1966 letter, Buffett explained the investment in BH and told his partners of the "excellent management" and that "Berkshire is a delight to own... we are most fortunate to have Ken Chace running the business in a first-class manner, and we also have several of the best sales people in the business heading up this end of their respective divisions."

8. Buffett would be the only one who could allocate capital

Given the company's history of pouring money into textiles, Buffett needed control of capital. He had the flexibility of mind and knowledge of other industries to be able to allocate across a much wider landscape and make good investments with this money.

The first two years

The first two years Buffett was in charge of the company, BH was profitable. Very little cash was invested in the mills, despite

Ken Chace coming up with nice looking projections for possible investment in the business. Buffett could not see why the historic average return of BH, which was appalling, didn't represent the future return.

Chace managed to do as he had been asked and released capital tied up in inventories and non-current assets. Dividends were at first meagre and then non-existent, thus saving cash.

Some operations were so heavily loss-making that it was obvious to everybody it would be folly to continue, such as the fine lawn cotton division, which accounted for about 10% of the firm's output. This was stopped, with the loss of hundreds of jobs.

By early 1967, cash had accumulated to such an extent that the 1966 annual report hinted at potential additional legs for the firm's future income: "The Company has been searching for suitable acquisitions within, and conceivably without, the textile field."

We will move on to look at one such brilliant deal in the next chapter.

Learning points

1. **Don't get emotional**. Buffett's anger led him to control 70% of a business that was going down a hole. He then had to dig his way out – he did it expertly and had some good luck, and so all ended well. But it would have been even better if he started with raw material of a high grade.

2. **Management of high ability and integrity are crucial**. It is wise business practice to make sure important people are well motivated, linked to which, targets and financial rewards packages should be kept simple (a couple of sentences will do – remuneration consultants' multi-page reports on incentive packages are not required) and lucrative if shareholders are served well.

3. **Reallocate capital**. A business does not need to invest in its own industry. Higher returns on capital employed may be available elsewhere.

4. **Try to behave decently with all who you come into contact with**. There were many points in the 20 years after 1965 that the cold-hearted rational thing to do with Berkshire Hathaway would have been to close the operating business and allocate the capital it used to more productive investments. But Buffett committed to the long term and stayed loyal to the workforce. His reputation for decency, while born of his inherently generous nature, rather than being affected, is an important business asset. Many families who wanted to sell their businesses have found a welcoming home within the Berkshire family, where continuity, long-term value and integrity have always been important watchwords, and where asset-stripping and other forms of short-termism were anathema. Dozens of family members still loyally run these companies today despite selling their shares to Berkshire decades ago. They are multi-millionaires but like working with their friend Warren Buffett, who offers them freedom to manage, respect, praise and a sense of purpose.

Investment 11

NATIONAL INDEMNITY INSURANCE

Summary of the deal

Deal	National Indemnity Insurance
Time	1967–present day
Price paid	$8.6m
Quantity	Whole company
Sale price	Currently worth billions of dollars
Profit	Billions of dollars

Let's have a recap of where we are up to. We have got to the point in the story (1965–1967) where Buffett's fund, the Buffett Partnership, had in the region of $30m–$60m of assets. Of this, Buffett's ploughed-back fees amounted to a fifth or so. The partnership was the majority shareholder in a rubbish business producing commoditised textiles, Berkshire Hathaway (BH), with about $22m of net assets and a similar market capitalisation. BH managed to generate some profit in this period, but it was clear to Buffett that the enterprise would never produce satisfactory returns on capital employed over the long run.

Buffett gave instructions that all capital investment in textiles had to be approved by him, and money was to be released from inventory and receivables as much possible while allowing the mills to stay open. Buffett was hesitant to close the mills so long as the managers and workers were willing to try to produce profits – this went on for 20 years.

Buffett's time was largely devoted to looking for new investments for the partnership fund, but he also had to think about what to do with BH. He regularly talked on the phone to Ken Chace, president of BH, to discuss where money could be shaved from BH's operations.

Jack Ringwalt

Very early on in the life of the investment partnerships, in the mid-1950s, Buffett had approached a well-known Omahan and enticed him to invest some of his money. This was Jack Ringwalt, who had made his fortune by growing an insurance company from scratch. Despite Buffett looking like a teenager, Ringwalt offered to invest $10,000 with him. Buffett rejected this and said that Ringwalt should place $50,000, as he would accept nothing less!

Ringwalt, a college drop-out and shrewd businessman said, "If you think I am going to let a punk kid like you handle $50,000 of my money, you are even nuttier than I thought."[23] He rescinded his $10,000 offer. A few years later he ruminated on what that $50,000 would have become in Buffett's hands and he concluded that it would have reached $2m after 20 years.

Through the 1950s and early 1960s, Buffett watched from a distance as Ringwalt's National Indemnity Insurance Corporation went from strength to strength. Finally, in February 1967 Buffett was in a position to benefit from the future growth of this well-run company. Its purchase was to transform Berkshire Hathaway and put it on the road to greatness.

National Indemnity in 1967

Jack Ringwalt started National Indemnity (NICO) with his brother, Arthur Ringwalt, in 1940 when he discovered that two Omaha taxi companies were unable to get liability insurance elsewhere. NICO initially had four employees, including the brothers. They could see an enormous potential in supplying insurance for non-standard risks – those areas that the large insurance groups stayed away from. The philosophy that there is a proper premium rate for every legitimate risk was captured in Jack Ringwalt's aphorism, "There's no such thing as a bad risk. There are only bad rates."

This means that *risky* insurance classes such as long-haul trucks, taxis, rental cars and public buses should not be arbitrarily rejected – just so long as the premiums were sufficiently high to justify the risk. NICO went much further than insuring vehicles and covered some quite unusual items, including:

- Lion tamers and other circus performers.

- Burlesque stars' legs.

- Radio station treasure hunts – NICO paid out if someone found the hidden item after following cryptic clues.

Jack Ringwalt was renowned for his penny pinching, such as habitually turning off lights and not taking his coat at lunchtime in case he had to pay to have it looked after in a cloakroom. These are the sort of habits a true value seeker displays and, as such, it should be no surprise that Ringwalt was just the sort of person Buffett liked. Ringwalt was likeable in other respects too, such as his intelligence and business knowledge. He knew when to take a risk and when to back away – the odds had to be right. Ringwalt and Buffett became friends.

By February 1967, National Indemnity was writing so much insurance that it built up a float of $17.3m. This is money received in premiums but not yet paid out in claims or operating expenses.

If the premiums kept rolling in and underwriting discipline was maintained (that is, insurance policies were not underpriced) the insurance float would remain at $17.3m or even grow.

Ringwalt regarded himself as a good investor and sought places to invest that float, providing another source of income for the firm. Buffett thought he could do better than Ringwalt. He figured that if the underwriting business merely broke even or made a small loss, he could make good money out of NICO simply by investing a proportion of the float in shares.

As usual, Buffett felt a need to widen his circle of competence to encompass the insurance business. Thus he spent a long time in libraries researching the mechanisms and logic of insurance. Finally, he approached Ringwalt to try to get him to sell NICO.

The National Indemnity deal

The National Indemnity deal would probably never have happened if it wasn't for another Omahan, Charles Heider, an Omaha stockbroker who competed with Buffett in the early 1950s; they both went out to persuade wealthy people to buy shares through the brokers they worked for.

Heider had so much respect for Buffett that he was one of the first to join his investment partnerships. While Buffett was the upstart, building up the fund in the 1960s, Heider was well-established and well-respected in Omaha. They conversed from time to time. One of the things they talked about was Jack Ringwalt and National Indemnity, as Heider was a director of NICO. He told Buffett that there were times when Ringwalt became exasperated with the whole business – usually after a customer claim had annoyed him – and at those moments he felt like giving up and selling the whole thing. But Heider said that Ringwalt had these moments of exasperation for only 15 minutes or so each year.

This was music to Warren's ears. He said that Heider should phone him the next time Ringwalt was in a mood to sell. In the meantime, Buffett asked Ringwalt to send him the same information he was sending out to the small number of outside shareholders. Ringwalt mistakenly thought that Buffett was flattering him by showing an interest in how NICO managed its investment float. He thought Buffett might want to learn from him about what shares to invest in and he agreed to send Buffett the information. Of course, what Buffett was really interested in was the operations of the business and he gained an impression of many years of the business' history from the material Ringwalt sent him.

February 1967

Charlie Heider had a reputation for shifting blocks of shares and in early 1967 he received a phone call from Jack Ringwalt asking if it was possible for him to sell the firm for $10m. As he had promised, Heider immediately called his friend Warren Buffett. A meeting was set up that very afternoon. The meeting was short – Ringwalt was on his way home and then going on holiday the next day. Buffett quizzed him about the sale, as follows:

WB: "How does it happen you never sold your company?"

JR: "Because crooks and bankrupt people have wanted it."

WB: "What other reason?"

JR: "I would not want the other stockholders to take less per share than I would receive myself."

WB: "What else?"

JR: "I wouldn't want to double-cross my agents."

WB: "What else?"

JR: "I don't want my employees to worry about losing their jobs."

WB: "What else?"

JR: "I am sort of proud of this as an Omaha institution and I would want it to remain in Omaha."

WB: "What else?"

JR: "I don't know – isn't that enough?"

WB: "What is your stock worth?"

JR: "According to the *World-Herald* [Omaha newspaper], the market value is $33 per share, but the stock is worth $50 per share."

WB: "I will take it."[24]

Ringwalt had not expected that – he had no idea that Buffett wanted to buy the company. He had also calmed down and was moving back towards a mood where he was not sure he wanted to sell the business. Ringwalt later said, "I thought, however, that Mr. Buffett at least had an honest reputation and was financially responsible and that it might not be such a bad idea. I felt in addition that he would probably change his mind while I was in Florida anyhow."[25]

But Buffett was very sure. Within the week he had documents prepared (a contract no more than one page long) and funds deposited ready for payment – he did not want any delays that might allow Ringwalt to change his mind. Indeed, Buffett thought that Ringwalt had wanted to change his mind, but he also knew him to be an honest man and that he would not back out of deal – although he did try to deter Buffett from buying for a short time.

Ringwalt signed more or less as soon as he returned from holiday. He turned up to the meeting ten minutes late and ever since the joke has been that he was driving around looking for a meter with some time left on it, ever the penny-pincher. The rumour is that in reality he was still unsure about selling. Berkshire Hathaway purchased the company for $8.6m.

Buffett in control of National Indemnity

Buffett has a wonderful knack for holding on to very talented and experienced people. He doesn't mind that they are getting on in years; their knowledge, judgement and contacts are often vital to the success of the enterprise. Besides, he has numerous investments to think about; he simply cannot deal with the day-to-day detail of running any one company.

He persuaded Jack Ringwalt to stay and work for the company. Buffett paid him well and cultivated their friendship. Ringwalt thought that he was in for a 30-day transition period, but ended up staying for six years. He said, "I found Mr Buffett to be a very considerate Chairman of the Board and I did remain with the Company for more than six years, at which time I was well beyond the normal retirement age of 65."[26] Wisely, Ringwalt used some of the cash he received from the sale of NICO to buy shares in Berkshire Hathaway, and thus made another fortune.

Did NICO have a competitive advantage?

In considering NICO's competitive advantage, let's start by looking at an extract from Buffett's 2004 letter to Berkshire Hathaway shareholders:

"When we purchased the company – a specialist in commercial auto and general liability insurance – it did not appear to have any attributes that would overcome the industry's chronic troubles. It was not well-known, had no informational advantage (the company has never had an actuary), was not a low-cost operator, and sold through general agents, a method many people thought outdated. Nevertheless, for almost all of the past 38 years, NICO has been a star performer. Indeed, had we not made this acquisition, Berkshire would be lucky to be worth half of what it is today.

What we've had going for us is a managerial mindset that most insurers find impossible to replicate. Take a look at the [table].

Portrait of a disciplined underwriter

National Indemnity Company

Year	Written premiums ($m)	Employees, year end	Ratio operating expenses to written premiums	Underwriting profit (loss) as a percentage of premiums
1980	79.6	372	32.3%	8.2%
1981	59.9	353	36.1%	(0.8%)
1982	52.5	323	36.7%	(15.3%)
1983	58.2	308	35.6%	(18.7%)
1984	62.2	342	35.5%	(17.0%)
1985	160.7	380	28.0%	1.9%
1986	366.2	403	25.9%	30.7%
1987	232.3	368	29.5%	27.3%
1988	139.9	347	31.7%	24.8%
1989	98.4	320	35.9%	14.8%
1990	87.8	289	37.4%	7.0%
1991	88.3	284	35.7%	13.0%
1992	82.7	277	37.9%	5.2%
1993	86.8	279	36.1%	11.3%
1994	85.9	263	34.6%	4.6%
1995	78.0	258	36.6%	9.2%
1996	74.0	243	36.5%	6.8%
1997	65.3	240	40.4%	6.2%
1998	56.8	231	40.4%	9.4%

Year	Written premiums ($m)	Employees, year end	Ratio operating expenses to written premiums	Underwriting profit (loss) as a percentage of premiums
1999	54.5	222	41.2%	4.5%
2000	68.1	230	38.4%	2.9%
2001	161.3	254	28.8%	(11.6%)
2002	343.5	313	24.0%	16.8%
2003	594.5	337	22.2%	18.1%
2004	605.6	340	22.5%	5.1%

Can you imagine *any* public company embracing a business model that would lead to the decline in revenue that we experienced from 1986 through 1999? That colossal slide, it should be emphasized, did not occur because business was unobtainable. Many billions of premium dollars were readily available to NICO had we only been willing to cut prices. But we instead consistently priced to make a profit, not to match our most optimistic competitor. We never left customers – but they left us."

To expand on Buffett's words: many insurers lose money because they chase after business, driving down the premiums they charge. Managers of these companies are often reluctant to forgo volume and market share. They want to keep the staffing levels high so they drive volume of business up. This makes insurance profits cyclical, because when insurers lose money from badly priced policies many go bust or are forced to cut back, leading eventually to raised premiums and the start of another cycle.

Buffett helped to break the normal mentality by saying that compulsory redundancies would not be imposed if volume of business fell due to a reluctance to follow competitors in silly low pricing. There was a short-term cost to this, but the benefit to the firm in terms of the culture of long-term profitability was very valuable. Underwriting discipline is superb at National Indemnity. This means that the float comes at no cost because the underlying insurance business makes profits or only small losses year by year.

The combination of a growing pot of no-cost float and Buffett's investing prowess applied to that float is a very important factor in his success. As Buffett says, it is no accident that much of the Berkshire Hathaway business is insurance.

Buffett's verdict on the National Indemnity deal – a "blunder"

Buffett referred to the way in which he went about the National Indemnity deal as a more serious blunder than the purchase of Berkshire Hathaway, saying it became "the most costly in my career". This self-deprecation – written in his 2014 letter to BH shareholders – needs some explanation. The key to understanding this logic is that his prime responsibility – and he felt it very keenly – was to his partners. The fund was 100% partnership money. If there was value in anything bought for the fund then his partners would obtain 100% of the benefit. So, if National Indemnity was a great buy, and Buffett could get the seller to part with all of it, and the partnership bought all of it, the partners would benefit 100% (less Buffett's fees, of course).

But Buffett erred here: instead of buying National Indemnity for the partners directly, he got Berkshire Hathaway to buy it. In February 1967, the partners owned a mere 61% of Berkshire Hathaway. Thus 39% of the value flowing from National Indemnity – and there was plenty of value – flowed to people other than the partners.

"So why did I purchase NICO for Berkshire rather than for BPL? I've had 48 years to think about that question, and I've yet to come up with a good answer. I simply made a colossal mistake… I opted to marry 100% of an excellent business (NICO) to a 61%-owned terrible business (Berkshire Hathaway), a decision that eventually diverted $100 billion or so from BPL partners to a collection of strangers."[27]

On the bright side, Buffett made those "strangers" (the other BH shareholders) very wealthy and he still made his partners very wealthy as well. And National Indemnity grew to be a world-beating success story.

Learning points

1. **The investor should be prepared to observe a good company for years before buying**. Do the analysis and put it on your watch list. Have a valuation in mind. If the opportunity arises then you can invest with discipline intact. If the opportunity never arises then use your money elsewhere, where you can invest with a margin of safety.

2. **The float held by insurance companies can be invested to make a fortune**, even if the underwriting business breaks even or makes a small loss. Those confident in their investing skills can pick up a number of insurance companies to obtain even more float. This is exactly what Buffett did.

3. **Hold on to a good thing for decades**. The original NICO business has been retained and expanded over the last five decades. There was never a thought of selling it. This is still a thriving business but it has been overshadowed by the amazing success of its reinsurance business (insuring insurers).

Investment 12

HOCHSCHILD-KOHN

Summary of the deal

Deal	Hochschild-Kohn
Time	1966–9
Price paid	$4.8m
Quantity	80% of the company's shares
Sale price	$4.0m
Loss	$0.8m

In the late 1960s, the 30-something Buffett was a multi-millionaire. For many years he had been entitled to 25% of the gain he made for his investment partners above the threshold of 6%. Because he averaged returns of around 30% per year and the investment fund had grown to more than $50m, he was able to both please his partners and earn himself millions each year.

Buffett's income was generally ploughed back into the partnership, thus he held a larger percentage of the partnership year by year. The partnership held about 70% of the struggling Berkshire Hathaway and by now BH had bought the insurance company,

National Indemnity, for $8.6m. Buffett firmly limited further significant investment in textiles.

Berkshire Hathaway was not alone in having the majority or all of its shares controlled by the Buffett Partnership: Hochschild-Kohn was another major investment around this time.

Hochschild-Kohn

In January 1966, an investment banking friend, David 'Sandy' Gottesman, mentioned to Warren Buffett the opportunity to buy a suffering Baltimore department store. Hochschild-Kohn was not competitive and needed a great deal of investment to initiate a revamp. It was privately owned by members of the Kohn family. Very few of the next generation wanted to be involved in running the business and they knew that it was unlikely to pay the family much in the way of dividends. Martin Kohn, CEO, told Gottesman that they were willing to sell, and a "discounted price" would be acceptable.

Buffett knew from the outset that he was buying "a second-class department store at a third-class price". But he liked the look of the net asset level on the balance sheet (which was more than the market capitalisation) and the hidden assets: unrecorded real estate values and a significant LIFO (last in, first out) inventory cushion, meaning that older stock was valued at older prices rather than the current price of replacement.

The deal

Warren Buffett and Charlie Munger met the Kohns and liked them. On the basis of the strength of the balance sheet they made an offer to buy all the shares. Louis Kohn agreed to run the business. They bought it in March 1966 through a new company, set up to hold the shares, called Diversified Retailing Company, Inc. The name of this new company gave a clue as to Buffett and Munger's intentions: they were going to build a retail group. The Buffett Partnership bought 80% of Diversified Retailing shares, with Charlie Munger's investment partnership, Wheeler, Munger, and Company, buying 10%, and Gottesman's fund buying 10%. The price of Hochschild-Kohn was $12m, with about half of that sum borrowed by the holding company, Diversified Retail.

Wheeler, Munger and Company was based in California and was independent of Buffett – but Munger and Buffett spoke daily on the telephone and had many investees in common. Wheeler, Munger and Company ran from 1962 to 1975 and produced average annual returns of 19.8%, much more than the returns from the Dow Jones Average, which gave only 5% per year in this period.

The importance of good people once again

In Buffett's 1966 half-year letter to partners he wrote about Hochschild-Kohn: "We have topnotch people (both from a personal and business standpoint) handling the operation... they will continue to run the business as in the past." He went on to emphasise the extreme weight he placed on managerial talent: "Even if the price had been cheaper but the management had been run-of-the-mill, we would not have bought the business."

How did things turn out?

In the summer of 1967, Buffett described the progress of Hochschild-Kohn as highly satisfactory. Ironically, considering its future success, in the same letter he was quite depressed about Berkshire Hathaway.

In January 1968, Buffett stated he was enjoying working with the leaders of companies that the partnership controlled, and that he was determined to keep a substantial proportion of the partnership's money in companies where he had control of all or the majority of the shares, even if that meant a reduction in his annual return target:

> "The satisfying nature of our activity in controlled companies is a minor reason for the moderated investment objectives discussed in the October 9th letter [changed from 10 percentage points over the Dow Jones Index to the lesser of 9% pa or a five percentage point advantage over the Dow]. When I am dealing with people I like, in businesses I find stimulating (what business isn't?), and achieving worthwhile overall returns on capital employed (say, 10–12%), it seems foolish to rush from situation to situation to earn a few more percentage points.
>
> It also does not seem sensible to me to trade known pleasant personal relationships with high grade people, at a decent rate of return, for possible irritation, aggravation or worse at potentially higher returns."[28]

Despite this general approach, Buffett left out Hochschild-Kohn (HK) from his list of praiseworthy performances; National Indemnity and Associated Cotton Shops (discussed in the next chapter) were picked out for honour, but the BH textile business and HK were not. Buffett had already vetoed managerial plans for HK to open further stores (after regretfully letting a store opening go ahead) to avoid throwing good money after bad.

Of the investment in HK, Munger said, "we were enough influenced by the Graham ethos that we thought if you just got enough assets for your dollars, somehow you could make it work out. And we didn't weigh heavily enough the intense competition between four different department stores in Baltimore."[29]

In 1968, store sales dropped significantly, and Buffett was on the lookout for a buyer for HK, or to liquidate the company. Fortunately, Supermarkets General was interested and purchased it in December 1969 for $5,045,205 of cash plus non-interest bearing Supermarkets General loan notes. Thus Diversified Retail, as well as receiving $5m into its bank account, became a holder of Supermarkets General debt, $2m of which was due for repayment in early 1970 and $4.54m due in early 1971. The present value (in 1969) of these notes approximated $6m so, effectively, Diversified Retail received about $11m on the sale. The cash received was kept in Diversified Retail. It still owed its creditors about $6m, roughly equal to the debt it owned in Supermarkets General.

The joint venture between Buffett's partnership fund, Charlie Munger's fund and Mr Gottesman's fund had made a small loss on the Hochschild-Kohn adventure. The problem with retail businesses is that the managers are usually under constant attack from competitors. If they come up with a good idea to enhance their offering, it won't be long before rivals have copied them. They have to be at the top of their game all the time. Also the constant innovation from competitors has to be matched.

As Buffett puts it, retail managers have to be "smart every day", whereas in other industries the managers do not destroy the business even if they perform in a mediocre fashion for a period. Thus it is that brands such as the *Washington Post,* Coca-Cola and Disney maintain the largest part of their franchises (their position in customer's minds) even if they have poor managers for a year or two. Department stores do not have that luxury. Of course, there are exceptional retailers out there who are smart every day and do beat competitors year after year, but they are rare.

Learning points

I'll let Buffett's reflections tell us what we should learn from this case. In his 1989 letter to Berkshire Hathaway shareholders he mused on his change in emphasis from the quantitative (balance sheet, in particular), to the qualitative, a thought prompted in part by the mistake of buying Hochschild-Kohn.[30]

"Shortly after purchasing Berkshire, I acquired a Baltimore department store, Hochschild-Kohn... I bought at a substantial discount from book value, the people were first-class, and the deal included some extras – unrecorded real estate values and a significant LIFO inventory cushion. How could I miss? So-o-o – three years later I was lucky to sell the business for about what I had paid. After ending our corporate marriage to Hochschild-Kohn, I had memories like those of the husband in the country song, 'My Wife Ran Away With My Best Friend and I Still Miss Him a Lot.' "

It is evident from this passage that Buffett has realised quantitative investment factors were not sufficient to make a great investment. He increasingly began to focus on qualitative factors as his career developed.

Some further reflections following the HK deal are as follows:

1. **It's far better to buy a wonderful company at a fair price than a fair company at a wonderful price**. Look for first-class businesses led by first-class management.

2. **Good jockeys will do well on good horses, but not on broken-down nags**. Both Berkshire's textile business and Hochschild-Kohn had able and honest people running them. The same managers employed in a business with good economic characteristics would have achieved fine records. But they were never going to make any progress while running in quicksand. Buffett said that when a management with a reputation for brilliance tackled a business with a reputation for bad economics, it would be the reputation of the business that remained intact.

3. **Avoid businesses with problems**. Buffett has said that he and Munger have not learned how to solve difficult business problems, but they have learned how to avoid them. In business and investment it is usually far more profitable to

simply stick with the easy and obvious than it is to resolve the difficult. On occasion, a great investment opportunity occurs when a great business is faced with a single large, but solvable, problem. This was the case at American Express and GEICO, as we saw in earlier chapters.

4. **The overwhelming importance in business of the unseen force, the institutional imperative**. Buffett said he had seen that, "(1) As if governed by Newton's First Law of Motion, an institution will resist any change in its current direction; (2) Just as work expands to fill available time, corporate projects or acquisitions will materialize to soak up available funds; (3) Any business craving of the leader, however foolish, will be quickly supported by detailed rate-of-return and strategic studies prepared by his troops; and (4) The behavior of peer companies, whether they are expanding, acquiring, setting executive compensation or whatever, will be mindlessly imitated." He tried to organise and manage his investments so as to minimise the influence of this institutional imperative. One way of achieving this was to go into business with people whom he liked, trusted and admired.

5. **Buffett was born neither an investor nor a businessman**. He learned through experience, both personal and vicarious, how things work. The learning process took decades to get to a reasonably high standard and still mistakes were made. An interest in lifelong learning is a prerequisite for an investor. Buffett's openness to correction has meant that he has made a sufficient number of good calls to produce a superior performance overall.

Investment 13

ASSOCIATED COTTON SHOPS

Summary of the deal

Deal	Associated Cotton Shops
Time	1967–present day
Price paid	Uncertain, but $6m has been mentioned
Quantity	80% of the company's shares
Sale price	Uncertain as it was merged with Berkshire Hathaway in the 1970s
Profit	Good, but not separately identifiable

By 1967, Buffett was running a very unusual investment fund. Rather than following convention by only taking minority stakes in stock market quoted companies, he had positioned his partnership as the majority shareholder of a broken textile company, Berkshire Hathaway (with an insurance subsidiary soon to be added). In addition, $4.8m of the partners' money (about 10% of the fund) was used to buy an 80% stake in a brand new company called Diversified Retail, and he became Diversified's Chief Executive Officer. This organisation borrowed an additional $6m and purchased the department store business Hochschild-Kohn in 1966.

Then in early 1967 Buffett and the minority shareholders in Diversified Retail agreed to expand the retail empire by buying Associated Cotton Shops, a dress shop chain.

The business

Associated Cotton Shops was started in 1931 by Benjamin Rosner (with Leo Simon, who died in the mid-1960s), with a single shop in Chicago, using only $3,200. Thirty-six years later it had annual sales of $44m and 80 stores. It had shops in inner-city areas, many of which were pretty tough (staff were constantly on the lookout for shoplifters). Rosner, 63 in 1967, was a renowned penny-pincher and a workaholic – qualities Buffett greatly admired. There is a great story about Rosner that Buffett likes to relate. It emphasises his admiration for Rosner's obsession with the business and how he, like Buffett, beats to a different drum. It is as follows.

Rosner attended a black tie dinner, where he was engrossed in conversation with another businessman about the minutiae of their businesses. He was keen to find out if he was getting the best price on rolls of toilet paper – standard fancy-dinner conversation, you understand. The other chap revealed that he was paying more for his toilet paper than Rosner. Instead of being pleased, Rosner was worried: it could mean that the supplier was cheating him by sending him slightly smaller rolls, while pretending they were the same. He immediately left the dinner, went to his warehouse and spent the rest of the evening counting the number of sheets on a roll. Sure enough, he found that there were fewer sheets to a roll than normal!

The deal

When they first began to discuss a possible deal, Rosner offered to show Buffett around a few stores so he could see what he might be buying. Buffett turned him down flat. The details of retailing were beyond his circle of competence. But what was definitely within his circle was the financial situation of the company then and in the recent past. So he asked Rosner to read the previous five years of balance sheet data over the phone.

At a meeting, with Charlie Munger present, Rosner was impatient and keen to conclude a deal quickly. So after about half an hour of discussion he said to Buffett, "They told me that you were the fastest draw in the West! Draw!" Buffett replied that he would not delay much longer and that a decision would be made that very afternoon – all the men in the room knew when to be decisive. It is not clear how much was paid for Associated Cotton Shops, but a figure of $6m has been mentioned in some sources.

Afterwards

Rosner sold because he wanted to retire, but Buffett asked him to stay on to help the transition. He knew all along that Rosner wouldn't be able to quit. Remarkably, he ended up staying with the firm for another 20 years. He later told his friend Buffett why it worked: "You forgot you bought this business. And I forgot I sold it." You can't get more of a tribute to Buffett's hands-off managerial style than that, though it is only a tribute if the managers excel in such conditions.

Buffett greatly praised Rosner, which must have helped retain him. But despite the "forgot you bought this business" quip, Buffett was very keen on receiving monthly reports on how the business was operating. While he felt he had no eye for retail, Buffett had a very sharp eye for financials.

Rosner's performance was very pleasing. Buffett wrote to partners in January 1968 that the acquisition "couldn't be more gratifying. Everything was as advertised or better. The principal selling executive, Ben Rosner... continued to do a superb job." Six months later he wrote to partners that Ben Rosner, "continue[d] to meld effort and ability into results." For 1968 as a whole Buffett put the return on capital employed in Associated Cotton Shops at about 20%.[31]

During 1969, Associated Cotton Shops was renamed Associated Retail Stores, and Buffett was very happy with how things had turned out:

> "Associated Retail Stores has a net worth of about $7.5 million. It is an excellent business with a strong financial position, good operating margins and a record of increasing sales and earnings in recent years. Last year, sales were about $37.5 million and net income about $1 million. This year should see new records in sales and earnings, with my guess on the latter to be in the area of $1.1 million after full taxes."[32]

So there you have it: the retail industry is a very difficult game to get right, but some people have a special talent for wringing out high rates of return on capital employed, and they can do it year after year. Buffett shrewdly nurtured the friendship of many great retailers in the decades that followed. We can think of the Blumkin family at Nebraska Furniture Mart, or the Friedman family at Borsheims, or Bill Child of RC Willey, for example.

Learning points

1. **Circle of competence**. We all have a circle of competence, but some people think their circle is much bigger than it really is. Buffett (and Munger) each define their circles quite narrowly. In other words they freely acknowledge that there are many subjects for which they have insufficient competence to be able to draw conclusions from data presented to them. For example, they never buy hi-tech companies because they cannot understand the prospects for the organisation ten years down the line. In fact, they regard most industries as lying outside of their circle of competence – they simply cannot analyse investments in those fields.

2. **It's great to partner with keen cost-cutters**. Ben Rosner knew his business inside out and he was in the habit of looking for ways to remove every ounce of fat from its operations every day. This resulted in very fine returns on capital employed.

3. **People value respect as much as financial reward**. After Ben Rosner sold the business he had more than enough money on which to retire, but he was enticed to continue working. He liked the mutual respect and trust between Buffett and himself. This was manifest in the freedom he was given to control his domain, the praise that was lavished upon him and the absolute trust Buffett placed in him not to behave in a way harmful to the interests of Buffett's partners.

Investment 14

INVESTING IN RELATIONSHIPS

Breathless, overexcited punting on shares seems to come in waves every few years. Each cycle, with its crash and its casualties, teaches *revelatory* lessons to those who pay little attention to stock market history. To wiser heads it reinforces the determination to remember to take a position to exploit the madness of the crowd, rather than to participate in the madness.

The 1960s rise in the market came on top of the 1950s boom. The hangover from the excitement caused many companies to go bust and many speculators to lose a bundle. How did Buffett see things at the time, between 1967 and 1969, and what did he do?

As we will see, Buffett went through a great deal of thought at this time about the stock market, how to value shares and the way in which he wanted to engage with company managers on a personal level. This chapter is not about a particular financial investment, but instead about a challenging period in Buffett's career where he had to make some big and difficult decisions. It helps inform us about the evolution of his investment style during these years.

Go-go years

The two decades following the Great Depression were years when the almost universal advice was: do not touch shares, they are dangerous, by nature speculative. This attitude held down share prices until the early 1950s. There were many bargains to be had at the time. Then, as companies proved that the good economic times fed through into rising profits and dividends, share prices rose.

The mood shifted and many people began to feel that shares were great things to own. *My friend doubled his money in a couple of years. He loves investing in the stock market. I'll jump in too.* This was a new generation who had experienced post-war prosperity and rising prices; 1929 was ancient history. The Dow Jones Industrial Average index (Dow) trebled from 200 to 600 in the 1950s and then rose another two-thirds between 1960 and 1966.

The average share was selling at a price of only 7.2 times the last reported annual earnings per share (this is a price-to-earnings ratio, or PE, of 7.2) in 1950. The PE is a commonly used measure of the cheapness or expensiveness of a share. In 1956 the PE was 12.1 – still a reasonably low level – allowing Buffett to find many companies that were cheap relative to their value to a private owner. In the 1960s however, the average price-to-earnings ratio was generally in the range of 15 to 21. This higher level made finding bargains more difficult, but not impossible.

As investors piled into sprawling conglomerates, and the electronic and chemical companies of tomorrow (Dustin Hoffman received advice on the 'industry of tomorrow' in *The Graduate* in 1967), Buffett grew increasingly anxious because he found few bargains for the partnership's money. He was running out of ideas as the market gained in euphoria.

Buffett was no ordinary fund manager

The first practical step Buffett took was to close the partnership to new investors in early 1966. He said: "I feel substantially greater size is more likely to harm future results than to help them. This might not be true for my own personal results, but it is likely to be true for your results."[33]

Note the contrast with many other fund managers. A booming market is an opportunity for them to earn substantially more in fees, as everyone wants to be in shares. Managers get a fee amounting to about 0.5% to 1% for every dollar/pound in the fund under management, which gives them an incentive to expand the funds they control.

Buffett created a different incentive structure. First, he had an innate sense of decency and honour, and would honestly try to do his best for his partners, many of whom were close friends or relatives. Second, Buffett had a distinctly unusual fee structure. He received nothing for his services unless he achieved a return of at least 6% each year. If he carried on buying shares he regarded as potentially overpriced merely to grow the fund under his management, there was no financial benefit for him.

Frustration and confusion in 1967

By early 1967, Buffett's flow of investment ideas – businesses he could actually buy – was down to a trickle. He was frustrated, confused even, with market behaviour. The market was in a manic phase, where fully priced to overpriced companies were commonplace. How could he invest, as opposed to speculate, in such an environment?

Buffett pondered this question long and hard. Should he join the crowd and go for short-term plays and the exciting *companies of tomorrow*, even if they lacked a profit history? Into this mix, a major factor was that he was already rich (to the tune of about $10m). Wasn't it about time he concentrated on other things in life, like his family?

Buffett's incomprehension

Buffett was so irritated by the market's odd behaviour in the late 1960s that he wanted to make it clear to his investors that the market can do some strange and irrational things. It cannot, therefore, be predicted over short periods, meaning months and even years. In his July 1966 letter to partners he repeated that he was "not in the business of predicting general stock market or business fluctuations". He said that if investors thought he could do this then they should not be in the partnership.

He never bought or sold shares on the basis of what other people thought the stock market would do. He emphasised again that he would only concentrate on what he thought the *company* would do. "The course of the stock market will determine, to a great degree, when we will be right, but the accuracy of our analysis of the company will largely determine whether we will be right. In other words, we tend to concentrate on what should happen, not when it should happen."[34]

A few months later in his January 1967 letter, Buffett tried to convince his followers that the ten years of the partnership were a very special period, giving unrepeatable returns, averaging 29.8% per year. He said, there was "absolutely no chance" of this being duplicated, or even remotely approximated, during the next decade. Diminishing investment performance would come about because of the scarcity of ideas – all he could do was try to "utilize those [ideas] available more intensively"[35]. Even with that increased intensity, there was a real danger that "a trickle has considerably more chance of drying up completely than a flow".[36]

Buffett believed that two ingredients were now missing.

He was no longer a "hungry twenty-five-year-old working with $105,100 initial partnership capital".[37] He was now a "better fed" 36-year-old who had the difficulty of investing a much larger amount of money: $54,065,345. He had to buy in larger amounts to move the dial of performance and this cut down the number of possible companies because not many had a sufficiently large free float (shares held by investors other than those closely connected with the firm, e.g. founding family or directors).

Second, the market environment was no longer conducive to successful implementation of his investment philosophy. Compared with 1956, there were only "one-fifth to one-tenth" as many really good investment ideas coming out of the application of his philosophy. At the beginning of the partnership, in a market environment of much lower share prices relative to assets and earnings, there were substantial numbers of companies selling significantly below the value to a private owner: 15 to 25 companies could be identified and Buffett could be "enthusiastic about the probabilities inherent in all holdings".[38] As he surveyed the scene in 1967 he found very few companies that were even understandable to him.

Things were so bad that Buffett declared that for the period 1964–66 he only identified two or three shares per year that had "an expectancy of superior performance".

What to do?

The one thing Buffett would not do was change the central elements of his philosophy (analyse businesses, margin of safety, aim for reasonable returns, exploit Mr Market). He would not step outside his circle of competence, or his "sphere of understanding". More specifically, Buffett rejected the popular approaches of the late 1960s:

He dismissed the notion of buying technology shares, "which is away over my head".[39]

He also dismissed the then popular approach of investing in shares "where an attempt to anticipate market action overrides business valuations"[40] despite well-publicised reports indicating that some individuals had performed this trick well and made quick profits. Buffett said, "It represents an investment technique whose soundness I can neither affirm nor deny. It does not completely satisfy my intellect (or perhaps my prejudices), and most definitely does not fit my temperament".[41]

Finally, he would not "seek out activity in investment operations, even if offering splendid profit expectations, where major human problems appear to have a substantial chance of developing."[42] After the experience of the Dempster Mill layoffs, with all its vitriol, and the harsh decisions at Berkshire Hathaway textiles regarding the labour force, Buffett could not stand the thought of tension and conflict arising in other companies that might need rationalising.

Misguided short-term performance measurement

To go along with a belief in divining short-term market or share movements, in the late 1960s there was a shift to short-term measures of success or failure as an investor. Buffett was upset with the possibility that people might insist he be held to account on short-term targets – after all, other fund managers were. Here is what Buffett said in his October 1967 letter to partners:

"For years I have preached the importance of measurement. Consistently I have told partners that unless our performance was better than average, the money should go elsewhere. In recent years this idea has gained momentum throughout the investment (or more importantly, the investing) community. In the last year or two it has started to look a bit like a tidal wave. I think we are witnessing the distortion of a sound idea. I have always cautioned partners that I considered three years a minimum in determining whether we were 'performing'. Naturally, as the investment public has taken the bit in its teeth, the time span of expectations has been consistently reduced to the point where investment performance by large aggregates of money is being measured yearly, quarterly, monthly, and perhaps sometimes even more frequently... The payoff for superior short-term performance has become enormous, not only in compensation for results actually achieved, but in the attraction of new money for the next round. Thus a self-generating type of activity has set in which leads to larger and larger amounts of money participating on a shorter and shorter time span. A disturbing corollary is that the vehicle for participation (the particular companies or stocks) becomes progressively less important – at times virtually incidental – as the activity accelerates."

Buffett's shift to embrace the qualitative (while not abandoning the quantitative)

In his early career, Buffett was strongly influenced by the ideas of Benjamin Graham, who focused particularly on net assets or, even more especially, the net current assets in the balance sheet, with some attention also directed at the earnings power and the qualitative factors of business prospects, quality of managers and stability of enterprise. Trumping everything else was the balance sheet strength due to the margin of safety it gave.

Buffett was tempted to try other approaches, tentatively at first and then more boldly. The success of Disney, American Express and a host of other investments made him want to put increasing amounts of money into companies with excellent qualitative characteristics – largely regardless of the net asset position.

However, this did not mean Graham's methods had to be completely abandoned and entirely substituted with a new approach. It is perfectly possible to run a portfolio using the ideas of Graham and the combined ideas of Philip Fisher, Charlie Munger and the 30-something Buffett, as this quote from Buffett's October 1967 letter to partners made clear:

"The evaluation of securities and businesses for investment purposes has always involved a mixture of qualitative and quantitative factors... Interestingly enough, although I consider myself to be primarily in the quantitative school, the really sensational ideas I have had over the years have been heavily weighted toward the qualitative side where I have had a 'high-probability insight'. This is what causes the cash register to really sing. However, it is an infrequent occurrence, as insights usually are, and, of course, no insight is required on the quantitative side – the figures should hit you over the head with a baseball bat. So the really big money tends to be made by investors who are right on qualitative decisions but, at least in my opinion, the more sure money tends to be made on the obvious quantitative decisions."[43]

Clearly, Buffett was not saying out with the old and in with the new; Benjamin Graham's way still has a great deal of validity. Despite this, it was wise to recognise that the 1950s was a particularly great time to be hunting for balance sheet bargains, when shares were so low that price-to-earnings ratios were in single digits and net assets or net current assets were frequently greater than market capitalisation. But this type of investment approach has drought years when the market is high. The quantitative bargains were disappearing in the late 1960s.

Buffett offered some potential explanations for why this happened:

- **Competing investors had jumped on the bandwagon**. Graham's books were popular, so others picked up on his ideas too. Buffett suggested that the constant combing and re-combing of investment lists had led to higher prices. What was really needed for this method to work again across a range of shares was "an economic convulsion such as that of the '30s to create a negative bias toward equities and spawn hundreds of new bargain securities".[44]

- **Takeover bids had become more commonplace** and these tend to focus on bargain issues, thus removing them from the market.

- **The large increase in the number of security analysts** who might bring forth "an intensified scrutiny of issues far beyond what existed some years ago"[45] whether or not they were Graham followers. There were now hundreds more analysts and fund managers, many of whom had cottoned on to the presence of undervalued shares, and therefore there were fewer neglected and unloved companies.

Buffett still saw the quantitative bargain as the *bread and butter* of his investment approach, but at that time there was a "virtual disappearance of the bargain issue as determined quantitatively".[46]

Even today, Buffett and Munger do not reject the idea of quantitative bargains as being a good way to gain high returns if you are investing small sums. It's just that when you are investing billions you can't find these bargains in big enough companies.

Easing back the commitment to the partnership

Buffett was so fed up with the new-era investing approach adopted by others in the market and the scarcity of bargains in 1967 that he penned a few sentences in his autumn letter of that year which came as a bombshell to his partners:

"When the game is no longer being played your way, it is only human to say the new approach is all wrong, bound to lead to trouble, etc. I have been scornful of such behavior by others in the past. I have also seen the penalties incurred by those who evaluate conditions as they were – not as they are. Essentially I am out of step with present conditions. On one point, however, I am clear. I will not abandon a previous approach whose logic I understand (although I find it difficult to apply) even though it may mean foregoing large and apparently easy, profits to embrace an approach which I don't fully understand, have not practiced successfully and which, possibly, could lead to substantial permanent loss of capital."[47]

Personal motivation

Buffett realised that he did not want to keep working so hard. He was exhibiting obsessive behaviour. He would work all day and evening, neglecting his family. He had a deal with his wife that he would ease-back once he had made $8m–$10m. That target had been reached. He wrote:

> "Changed personal conditions make it advisable to reduce the speed of the treadmill. I have observed many cases of habit patterns in all activities of life, particularly business, continuing (and becoming accentuated as years pass) long after they ceased making sense... Elementary self-analysis tells me that I will not be capable of less than all-out effort to achieve a publicly proclaimed goal to people who have entrusted their capital to me. All-out effort makes progressively less sense."[48]

Buffett wanted more out of life both in terms of pursuing things other than money and in the type of investing he was doing. Instead of banging his head against the brick wall of a market in a speculative fever, he wanted to cut down his workload by focusing on businesses that he controlled, operated by people he liked, trusted and admired, even if this meant lower rates of return. He preferred to enjoy what he was doing, rather than make an unmitigated pursuit of financial returns:

> "I am likely to limit myself to things which are reasonably easy, safe, profitable and pleasant. This will not make our operation more conservative than in the past since I believe, undoubtedly with some bias, that we have always operated with considerable conservatism. The long-term downside risk will not be less; the upside potential will merely be less."[49]

He understood that many partners on reading this would be unwilling to accept the new lowered investment performance target, and would look elsewhere: "Partners with attractive alternative investment opportunities may logically decide that their funds can be better employed elsewhere, and you can be sure I will be wholly in sympathy with such a decision."[50]

On hearing this, a number of partners decided to withdraw money from the partnership to place it with fund managers who promised a more exciting future ($1.6m between October and December 1967). Buffett was pleased that these people had exited, because he was relieved "from pushing for results that I probably can't attain under present conditions."[51]

He outperformed – again

Ironically, just as Buffett was tiring of the stock market, this period was to produce some wonderful returns. The partnership gained 35.9% in 1967, compared with 19.0% for the Dow. After Buffett's management fee the return for partners was 28.4%, or $19,384,250 on net assets of $68,108,088. Buffett quipped this would "buy a lot of Pepsi". Buffett was a Pepsi drinker at the time, but would switch to Coca-Cola after buying a stake in the company.

Even so, Buffett could see through the artificiality of the gains. He referred to the rise as being caused by "speculative bonbons" fattening share traders. He knew it could all end in "indigestion" and "discomfort", even though he was being good and puritan by sticking to eating "oatmeal" – that is, following the Graham principles.[52]

Buffett noted that a large portion of the gains was achieved on one share that, after excellent growth in the period from 1964 to 1967, ended up being 40% of the portfolio. Even though he did not name it, we know, of course, that it was American Express, with a share price rise from around $38 to $180 at this time, making the partnership over $20m on a $13m investment.

While such a gain is nice to have, if you know anything about stock market history you know that picking one-off winners is not a sound basis on which to project forward your future returns. What matters is the availability of numerous investment opportunities, but there was no abundance at this time – there was a drought.

An end to the partnership?

Buffett was forced to confront the question of whether he was to quit running the partnership – understandably many partners had read his October 1967 letter and thought it signalled the start of the run-down. But, in January 1968, Buffett stated that the answer to this was, "Definitely, no." He said, "As long as partners want to put up their capital alongside of mine and the business is operationally pleasant (and it couldn't be better), I intend to continue to do business with those who have backed me since tennis shoes."[53]

The solution

So, in January 1968, Buffett thought he had found a compromise that would allow him to continue with less stress, less obsession, stronger relationships with his operational managers and with his family. He even agreed to help out on charitable endeavours, especially the civil rights movement. However, it was not long before he realised that the new portfolio of interests was simply not working out for him, as we'll see in the forthcoming chapters about later investment stories.

Learning points

1. **Markets go through periods of irrationality.**

2. **Stick with sound investing principles in good times and bad.**

3. **Life is not all, or even principally, about making money.** Human relationships matter.

4. **Most fund managers trying to pick shares to outperform the market will not do so if you take into account the high fees they are charging,** where these fees are unrelated to performance.

Investment 15

ILLINOIS NATIONAL BANK
AND TRUST

Summary of the deal

Deal	Illinois National Bank and Trust
Time	1969–80
Price paid	Approx. $15.5m
Quantity	97.7% of the bank's shares
Sale price	$17.5m plus 11 years of dividends estimated at over $30m
Profit	Over $32m, over 200%

Warren Buffett may have been wary of buying minority stakes in the go-go stock market of 1968–9, but he was excited by the prospect of picking up majority shareholdings in brilliantly organised businesses. After all, he had already experienced very pleasing outcomes from the purchases of National Indemnity and Associated Cotton Shops. Now these two businesses were throwing off cash for their parent, Berkshire Hathaway, why not use that cash to broaden Berkshire's portfolio of companies?

A profitable little bank

In 1931, Eugene Abegg, a young man with only $250,000 of capital, formed a bank in Rockford, Illinois. He named it Illinois National Bank and Trust Company, but many people just called it Rockford Bank, after the town. It had $400,000 of deposits. Since that time, no new capital had been added to the bank by its owners. Nevertheless, by 1969 Abegg had built, piece by piece, a bank with a net worth of $17m and $100m of deposits. It produced earnings of around $2m per year – a satisfactory return on capital employed. Ken Chace, president of Berkshire Hathaway, described such earnings as being "close to the top among larger commercial banks in the country" when measured as a percentage of deposits or total assets.[54]

As well as high returns on both assets/liabilities – earnings of 2% on $100m deposits, or $2m earnings on shareholders' funds of $17m ($2m/$17m = 11.8%) – the bank was conservatively run. It achieved its returns even though it took very little risk with the capital structure, liquidity and lending policy.

In banking it is easy to make the numbers look good for a while by borrowing excessively from financial markets to lend to high-risk prospects. Everything seems fine – until luck runs out. In contrast the Rockford Bank borrowed only infrequently from the capital or money markets, and it had a policy of maintaining a relatively high level of liquidity. This meant it had reserves of assets that it could turn into cash at short notice – rather than an excessive amount tied up in long-term lending – and it had access to short-term funds.

It was conservative in its lending too, with loan losses significantly below average. Furthermore, over 50% of its deposits were time deposits, creating greater stickiness in deposits held for customers. This lowers risk, but also reduces profits due to the higher interest rates paid. Given all of the safety-first policies it was surprising that the bank generated such high returns on capital. Buffett attributed this to excellent management.

The deal

Abegg, who owned one-quarter of the shares, had been in negotiation to sell the business to someone else before Buffett came along. The potential buyer had started criticising the deal and wanted an audit. This upset Abegg and he decided not to go ahead with that deal. Meanwhile, Buffett worked out what he was willing to pay, which turned out to be about £1m less than the other buyer.

Abegg was so fed up with the other bidders that he pressed his fellow shareholders to accept Buffett's offer, threatening to resign if they did not. Berkshire Hathaway bought 97.7% of the bank's shares in 1969. One well-informed observer, Robert P. Miles, quoted the buying price at $15.5m. Assuming that the number is correct, Buffett paid only seven times earnings for the largest bank in that town, which had demonstrated consistently high rates of return on capital employed. Even more remarkably, Eugene Abegg sold it at less than book value (net asset value).

In a very rare occurrence, Buffett decided to partly fund the purchase with $10m of borrowed money. He later said, "For the next three decades, we borrowed almost nothing from banks. (Debt is a four-letter word around Berkshire.)"[55]

The very pleasant Illinois National Bank experience

As we've already learned, Buffett liked to hold on to great managers to run his companies. He spotted the brilliance of Abegg very early on – he had shown time and again over 39 years running the bank that he really knew how to wring out returns and how to do so with low risk for shareholders. Despite Abegg being 71, Buffett was determined to get him to stay on – which was not very difficult as Abegg wanted to continue working.

Once he had got his man, Buffett adopted his usual light-touch style, leaving Abegg alone to manage the business operations. The following tribute shows that Buffett's faith was fully justified:

"Our experience has been that the manager of an already high-cost operation frequently is uncommonly resourceful in finding new ways to add to overhead, while the manager of a tightly-run operation usually continues to find additional methods to curtail costs, even when his costs are already well below those of his competitors. No one has demonstrated this latter ability better than Gene Abegg."[56]

Remarkably, in the five and a half years following the acquisition the bank paid Berkshire dividends of $20m – more than what it paid for the Rockford Bank shares. Furthermore, the value held within the bank franchise grew stronger over time.

How would you like to own this?

In 1971, the Illinois National Bank earned over 2% after tax on average deposits. Abegg did not slow down; he accelerated the efficiencies so that this rose to 2.2% in 1972. And the bank was expanding fast – in 1972 it increased loans to customers by 38%.

The next year was yet another record, with average deposits rising to $130m. Operating earnings after taxes were again at a high level for the industry, at 2.1% of average deposits.

In the 1975 BH letter to shareholders, Buffett highlighted the amazingly low level of bad loans at the bank: "It is difficult to find adjectives to describe the performance of Eugene Abegg, Chief Executive. Against average loans of about $65 million, net loan losses were $24,000, or 0.04%."[57]

Even that was to be bettered the next year, when loan losses fell to only 0.02% of outstanding loans, a very tiny fraction of the prevailing ratio in the banking industry in 1976. Note that through this period of rising profits, deposits (up $60m since 1969) and loans, the number of people employed by the bank remained at about the same level as at the time of purchase in 1969. With that team it expanded greatly into other activities such as trust, travel and data processing.

By 1977, earnings were $3.6m, giving a rate of earnings on assets about three times that of most large banks. Abegg was now 80 and asked Buffett if he could have some help. He was joined by Peter Jeffrey, formerly President and CEO of American National Bank of Omaha, as President and CEO.

And still they powered ahead, with a 2.1% return on assets in 1978. That is, net earnings after tax attributable to BH shareholders of $4.26m. In the period of a decade, consumer time deposits had quadrupled, net income had tripled and trust department income had more than doubled, while costs had been closely controlled.

But the Illinois National Bank had to go

In 1978, banking regulators told Buffett that he would have to separate the Rockford Bank from the rest of his businesses by the end of 1980. The regulators were tightening up on allowing banks to be part of non-banking organisations. Buffett announced that the most likely solution would be to spin it off to Berkshire shareholders sometime in the second half of 1980. In the meantime, Eugene Abegg and Peter Jeffery excelled themselves with a 2.3% return on assets ($5m) in 1979, trebling the level typically returned by competing banks.

The highest price is not always the best choice

In 1979, Buffett investigated the possibility of selling 80% or more of the banks' shares to an outside investor. He said, "We will be most choosy about any purchaser, and our selection will not be based solely on price. The bank and its management have treated us exceptionally well and, if we have to sell, we want to be sure that they are treated equally as well."[58] He still regarded a spin-off as a possibility if a fair price along with a proper purchaser could not be found by early autumn.

He bitterly resented losing the Illinois bank from the Berkshire stable, writing: "you should be aware that we do not expect to be able to fully, or even in very large part, replace the earning power represented by the bank from the proceeds of the sale of the bank. You simply can't buy high quality businesses at the sort of price/earnings multiple likely to prevail on our bank sale."[59]

The separation

On the last day of 1980, 41,086 shares of Rockford Bancorp Inc. (which owned 97.7% of Illinois National Bank) were exchanged for a like number of shares of Berkshire Hathaway – this meant the bank was valued as being worth roughly 4% of BH.

This method permitted all Berkshire shareholders, if they wanted, to maintain their proportional interest in the bank as well as their proportional interest in Berkshire. (There was an exception to this: Buffett himself was only allowed 80% of his proportional share by the bank regulators.) Berkshire's shares were trading at $425 each and therefore the bank was valued at $425 x 41,086, or $17.5m.

Alternatively, shareholders could end up with a disproportionate holding in the bank or in BH – they could swap some of their allocated bank shares for BH, or vice versa.

A tribute from Buffett

Unfortunately, Eugene Abegg died in July 1980. Buffett wrote of their friendship:

"As a friend, banker and citizen, he was unsurpassed.

You learn a great deal about a person when you purchase a business from him and he then stays on to run it as an employee rather than as an owner... From the time we first met, Gene shot straight 100% of the time – the only behavior pattern he had within him. At the outset of negotiations, he laid all negative factors face up on the table; on the other hand, for years after the transaction was completed he would tell me periodically of some previously undiscussed items of value that had come with our purchase...

Gene never forgot he was handling other people's money. Though this fiduciary attitude was always dominant, his superb managerial skills enabled the Bank to regularly achieve the top position nationally in profitability...

Dozens of Rockford citizens have told me over the years of help Gene extended to them. In some cases this help was financial; in all cases it involved much wisdom, empathy and friendship. He always offered the same to me. Because of our respective ages and positions I was sometimes the junior partner, sometimes the senior. Whichever the relationship, it always was a special one, and I miss it."[60]

Learning points

1. **Invest in outstanding businesses at reasonable prices**. If a business has shown high earnings power in the past and there is every reason to think that earnings power will grow, then it is worth paying a full price for the business.

2. **Even better, if you can get such a business at a low price then you will do very well**. Within a decade the Illinois National Bank had increased annual earnings by 150% to $5m, and probably quadrupled its value.

3. **Buy high proportions of great companies** – when Buffett found great companies like this, he bought as much of them as he could.

4. **It is a very good sign when a company founder cares greatly about who's buying the business** and not about selling out for every last penny he can get. Buffett knew that if the manager cared more about a high sale price and less about the management philosophy of the acquiring organisation, the chances are the merger would not work. Buffett acquired managers, like Eugene Abegg, or Ben Rosner of Associated Retail Stores, who would "run their businesses for Berkshire with every bit of the care and drive that they would have exhibited had they personally owned 100% of these businesses." This attitude should be "embedded in the character" of good managers.[61]

5. **Banks that stick to simple low-cost vanilla banking with an emphasis on low-risk and steady growth are a completely different prospect to complex banks** engaging in complex derivatives and market borrowing, and with investment bankers setting the culture.

6. **A manager continually looking to gain efficiencies and cost savings is one that is likely to be worth backing.** These actions continue to deepen and widen the moat of competitive advantage.

Investment 16

OMAHA SUN NEWSPAPERS

Summary of the deal

Deal	Omaha Sun Newspapers
Time	1969–80
Price paid	$1.25m
Quantity	All the company's shares
Sale price	Unknown, but likely to be a lot less than $1.25m
Profit	A financial loss, but a qualitative gain, including a Pulitzer Prize

B uffett started 1968 with partnership net assets of $68,108,088, having made a 35.9% return in 1967. But he was in a far from exuberant mood. The more the market was driven by speculative fever and accounting tricks, the more worried he became.

Buffett's attitude

It's important to understand Buffett's thinking. It was not satisfying for him to make money by watching his shares rise on the market. Satisfaction came from demonstrating that his analytical reasoning was sound. This was manifest through the performance of his chosen companies and the consequent rise in their share prices.

Logical analysis first, followed by business success, followed by share price rises. That is what made sense; the correct order of the investing universe. To witness a chosen investment rise 100% in a matter of weeks because promoters were pushing it for short-term goals was cause for concern, not for celebration. Gains made in irrationality can be quickly removed in an equally unreasonable manner.

The games people play

Buffett was thus fretful that the games being played would result in serious long-term damage to the socially important market mechanism of equity investment. Cynical manipulation would lead to failure and failure would lead to fear and loathing of the idea of investment in companies, which would reduce the flow of funds for vital businesses.

In his July 1968 letter to partners, Buffett wrote:

> "Spectacular amounts of money are being made by those participating (whether as originators, top employees, professional advisors, investment bankers, stock speculators, etc.) in the chain-letter type stock-promotion vogue. The game is being played by the gullible, the self-hypnotized, and the cynical."[62]

For the manipulation to work the promoters had to create illusions. The most popular way of doing this was through accounting numbers. Buffett said:

> "It frequently requires accounting distortions (one particularly progressive entrepreneur told me he believed in 'bold, imaginative accounting'), tricks of capitalization and camouflage of the true nature of the operating businesses

involved. The end product is popular, respectable and immensely profitable."[63]

While shaking his head at the madness of it all, Buffett at least had the comfort of making paper profits for his partners: "Quite candidly, our own performance has been substantially improved on an indirect basis because of the fallout from such activities... we have reaped market rewards much more promptly than might otherwise have been the case."[64] The partnership gained an astonishing $40m or 58.8% in 1968. In January 1969, Buffett handled $104m of assets.

Buffett kept a newspaper clipping of the crash in 1929 on his office wall as reminder of what comes from mania. Manias may seem like fun, but to play along with them can lead to a high risk of breaking Buffett's two most important rules of investing:

Rule 1: Don't lose money.

Rule 2: Don't forget rule number 1.

The Omaha Sun

Buffett, ever since his *Washington Post* delivery-round days, had a keen interest in quality journalism. Indeed, he relied on newspaper information to help develop his ideas. Both he and Charlie Munger had a great respect for analytical, critical, investigative journalism. Time is precious – what you choose to read can help to form character, as well as increase breadth and depth of knowledge.

The opportunity

In 1968, as Buffett shifted his focus to small companies he could control, he quite fancied the idea of becoming a newspaper proprietor, especially if the newspaper was selling at a reasonable price. Then the opportunity arose, in a very small way. His wife, Susie, knew Stanford Lipsey, the owner-publisher of the *Omaha*

Sun newspapers. One day Lipsey went to Buffett's office in Kiewit Plaza and said he wanted to sell.

The company produced half a dozen local-focused weekly newspapers in the greater Omaha area, with a total circulation of 50,000 and annual revenue of about $1m. These papers contained the usual local stories of goings-on in the neighbourhood. But they also investigated stories that the dominant publisher in Omaha, *Omaha World-Herald*, had missed or timidly chose not to print. Often these concerned the wrongheadedness and misdemeanours of those in local public office and other prominent Omahans.

Even Lipsey was only lukewarm about the business prospects of the papers, so it may be that Buffett was largely motivated by the important public service of probing and tough journalism rather than the investment opportunity. Either way, the deal was agreed in 20 minutes. Buffett later stated that he paid a million and a quarter for a company he expected to generate $100,000 p.a. that he could take out (this would equate to an 8% return on the invested capital). Lipsey remained as editor. An 8% return was lower than Buffett's usual expectation, but bear in mind that he could not find many other investment opportunities at the time, so a lot of the partnership's money was pretty idle.

There was another consideration here as well: Buffett had noticed that in some towns there was only one newspaper. This gave pricing power. By spending a million or so (about 1.5% of the partnership), Buffett could gain a foothold and some experience in publishing, which he hoped would stand him in good stead for future adventures (and it did). The transfer of ownership took place on 1 January 1969. All the shares were bought by Berkshire Hathaway.

Buffett, the Pulitzer Prize winner

Buffett, the proud controller of the *Omaha Sun* newspapers, with a small circulation and struggling to produce a target profit of

$100,000, had an intimate knowledge of his hometown. Into his possession came some information strongly indicating a scandal at one of the nation's favourite charities, based in Omaha.

Boys Town was established in 1917 by Father Flanagan, an Irish priest, as a refuge for homeless boys. By the mid-1930s it had 160 acres of land, a school and athletics facilities. It got a terrific boost when it was made famous in 1938 by being portrayed in an Oscar-winning film *Boys Town*, in which Spencer Tracy and Mickey Rooney starred. Following the film, the charity went national in its fund-raising, regularly sending out millions of letters. The letters implied that the boys would go hungry without more money and so money poured in. Boys Town expanded to 1,300 acres and by 1971 it housed 665 boys and employed 600 staff.

But things had started to sour

The boys were kept in a high degree of isolation – on campus, no contact with girls, only one (approved) visitor per month and their letters were censored. This was bad enough, but the main focus of Buffett and his editor at the Sun, Paul Williams, was how money was raised and spent.

In marketing to donors, Boys Town claimed it got no money from church, state or federal government. But, it turned out that the Nebraska state did supply funding. More investigations followed. Buffett enjoyed going around Omaha acting as a sleuth, alongside professional journalists. He helped compile the numbers on the charity. It was discovered that the 50m letters sent annually brought in so much money (about $25m a year) that the cash pile was growing at around $18m per year: four times what the charity spent. The pile had reached $209m (about $300,000 per boy), and still it pleaded for Americans to give generously. It even had two Swiss bank accounts. Also, Boys Town lacked financial control systems to manage the money it received – it had no plan of needed expenditure, or even a budget. Boys Town had mismanaged other people's money – which we know Buffett regarded as a great sin.

A scoop

The story was published in March 1972. It became a national scandal and all fundraising was halted. The next year, while the *Washington Post* won the Pulitzer for investigative reporting of the Watergate scandal, the little *Omaha Sun* won the prize for local investigative specialised reporting.

Sunlight as a disinfectant – Boys Town was reformed

From that point, Boys Town ramped up its spending on projects and was much more open about its finances. The board was changed, as was the administration. It opened the campus to consultants and switched to a home-family model for the boys where children lived in homes and were cared for by married couples. Today, Boys Town is a national leader in parenting and child speech-hearing impairment research and treatment, and gets a high rating for transparency.

But while Boys Town turned itself around, the *Omaha Sun* was failing financially. It was the poorly positioned second player in the town. When it was finally sold in 1980, the new Chicagoan owner could not make it work and the doors were closed in 1983. The rival, *Omaha World-Herald,* thrives to this day, covering local, national and international affairs.

Learning points

1. **There's more to life than short-term financial gain**. Buffett used a tiny proportion of his fund to back a newspaper that, at best, would produce a modest return. But sometimes it is worth investing in the future. Buffett has always said that he is a very lucky man. He has made so much money because he was fortunate enough to be born into a society with good

institutions: rule of law, property rights, a strong civil society, and checks and balances on power, including a free press. These things are precious; they allow us to thrive in freedom. Buffett might have regarded the use of 1.5% of the fund to help protect these institutions as a contribution to the cause. An expected return of 8% could have arisen as a bonus, but did not.

2. **Payment for education**. Buffett believed there were some excellent business franchises in American newspapers. In those days if you wanted to advertise your business, whether that be selling cars, houses or groceries, you were pretty well obliged to use the local rag. Most Americans lived in single-paper towns. A million and a quarter dollars tied up earning a low return to learn more about this business was a small price to pay. At this time, Buffett developed a preoccupation with finding out about the economics of newspapers and the details of their workings, which was similar to his earlier focus on understanding the insurance business inside out. This first step into the newspaper world later led to high returns at the *Buffalo Evening News*, and also a 20-fold return on a *Washington Post* investment. More recently, in 2012, BH bought 63 local papers.

3. **Hold on to good people**. Stan Lipsey became a good friend of Buffett's. He had great qualities as a man and as a newspaper publisher. A few years later, the *Buffalo Evening News* was in serious trouble. Stan Lipsey was the man Buffett persuaded to get it out of the mess. He headed *Buffalo Evening News* as Buffett's trusted key man for 32 years until 2012. On his retirement, Buffett was asked about the secret to Lipsey's success. "He's passionate about the newspaper," he replied. "He's 85, and he's always in motion – in a positive way. And he loves newspapers. You put that motion and passion together, and you have incredible results."[65]

4. **Don't forget the qualitative.** If anyone ever tells you that Buffett's success is purely down to his understanding of financial numbers and the financial markets, you'll know you are talking to someone who has not really understood him. People and relationships really matter to Buffett. Added to that, qualitative analysis, with all its slipperiness and imprecision, is central to gaining an edge.

Investment 17

MORE INSURANCE

Summary of the deal

Deal	Insurance and reinsurance
Time	1968–9
Price paid	Various small amounts
Quantity	N/A
Sale price	N/A
Profit	Considerable, but hidden within the Berkshire Hathaway holding company accounts

By 1969, the Buffett Partnership was becoming quite complex. The bulk of its money was invested in minority holdings of listed companies, but a substantial amount was invested in two major holdings. The first of these was Diversified Retailing (Associated Retail Stores), which was 80% owned by the partnership, with 10% owned by Charlie Munger's California-based investment fund and 10% owned by Sandy Gottesman's fund (First Manhattan Company).

The partnership also owned 70.3% of Berkshire Hathaway (691,441 shares out of 983,582). This company, under President Ken

Chace, had been transformed. Chace wrote to BH shareholders in early 1970 explaining what had happened: "Four years ago your management committed itself to the development of more substantial and more consistent earning power than appeared possible if capital continued to be invested exclusively in the textile industry."[66] He said that initially Buffett put the money released from textiles into marketable securities, "pending the acquisition of operating businesses meeting our investment and management criteria."[67] Chace could not have done this on his own. He needed Buffett to provide the impetus, to provide the analytical power, the competent eye roving over a wide range of industries, to shift money from textiles to other goods and services.

Chace was amazed to discover just how successful the strategy had been. The letter he wrote to BH shareholders in April 1970 pointed out that competitors had made a great mistake in narrowly framing themselves on a textiles-only strategy. He wrote, "firms which have continued to commit large sums to textile expansion" had produced "totally inadequate returns". In contrast, BH had made two major purchases of operating businesses. The boost that these two deals had given to BH meant that the company could achieve "an over-all return of more than 10% on average stockholders' equity last year in the face of a return of less than 5% from the portion of our capital employed in the textile business".

Thus, it can be deduced that the two acquired business must have produced a lot more than 10%. By then the textile business was using only around $16m of capital.

Berkshire Hathaway morphed into a holding company powerhouse

Over the two years of 1968 and 1969, Berkshire Hathaway sold its entire holdings of marketable securities, mostly shares, to hold much more cash, providing ammunition for future purchases of controlled companies. Happily, Chace was able to report that the company had made a profit on these securities of more than $5m after tax. Remember that as recently as 1965 BH had a market capitalisation of under $20m, a net asset value of $22m, and was barely producing profits from its one and only business, so a £5m uplift is quite something.

The gains provided important funds to facilitate the purchase of 97.7% of Illinois National Bank in 1969, which went on to produce terrific returns for the holding company (see Investment 15). This bank formed a strong pillar on which to build a business empire, alongside National Indemnity, which was bought in 1967 for $6.8m (money was taken from BH's textile operations for this). The insurance business produced another year of underwriting profit in 1969, so Buffett had the float of money at National Indemnity and its partner company, National Fire and Marine Insurance (bought in 1967), available for investment in securities at no cost. The insurance division of Berkshire Hathaway was also branching out, which Ken Chace described as follows:

"Our new surety department, although small, made good progress during the year. We are entering the workmen's compensation market in California through the establishment of a branch office in Los Angeles. Our new reinsurance division seems to be off to a strong start… We also have interesting plans for a new 'home state' insurance operation."[68]

For such a small company to be thinking of reinsurance already showed that Buffett and Chace thought big from a very early stage.

Some more companies added to the collection

BH also held the *Omaha Sun*, but that was financially insignificant. It then tacked on two further small companies in 1969. These were Blacker Printing Company (100% owned by BH), which was linked to the *Sun* newspaper, and Gateway

Underwriting Agency (70% owned by BH), which was a useful addition to the insurance division. Gateway acted (and still does) as a wholesale insurance agency connecting insurance agents with underwriting capacity.

By now Buffett had announced that his preference was to concentrate on majority-owned companies and so Chace stated that he did not anticipate "any further purchases of marketable securities" for Berkshire Hathaway. This was quite an interesting statement in light of the fact that Berkshire Hathaway later became famous for buying stock market traded shares such as *Washington Post* and Coca-Cola, and making a fortune from them. This is yet another indicator that building this business did not follow Buffett's grand plan so much as his *grand principles*, which led to different tactics at different times.

The grand principles included:

- Search for high rates of return on capital.

- Keep risks low, such as the risk with borrowing large amounts of money.

- Be an investor rather than a speculator; that is, analyse the business, look for reasonable returns and build in a margin of safety.

Capital uses

While there was about $16m tied up in textiles, the Illinois Bank had $17m of BH's net tangible assets, and the insurance company approximately $15m of BH's capital.

Putting the bank and insurance earnings together, Buffett estimated "their normal current earning power to be about $4 per share".[69] That was pretty good considering that the partnership had paid an average of $14.86 for each of its shares in BH.

Furthermore, Buffett judged that Diversified Retail and Berkshire Hathaway both had good prospects for future growth: "My personal opinion is that the intrinsic value of DRC and B-H will grow substantially over the years. While no one knows the future, I would be disappointed if such growth wasn't at a rate of approximately 10% per annum. Market prices for stocks fluctuate at great amplitudes around intrinsic value but, over the long term, intrinsic value is virtually always reflected at some point in market price. Thus, I think both securities should be very decent long-term holdings and I am happy to have a substantial portion of my net worth invested in them."[70]

Both Chace and Buffett made it plain that the search for acquisitions would continue.

Learning points

1. **Grand principles are more important than a grand plan**. Good return on capital employed from low-risk businesses obtainable at fair prices – these are important principles that can be applied in various ways. In applying them, Buffett and BH were taken in directions that could not have been foreseen at the outset.

2. **Intrinsic value is the focus of attention**. The market may move share prices away from intrinsic value for periods of time, but will eventually reflect it.

3. **Capital allocation was at the heart of Buffett's good investment performance**. Evaluation of companies in a number of industry sectors helped Buffett and his managers to escape a myopic focus on one type of firm only. Capital allocated to a company has an opportunity cost of capital calculated as the *next best use* return. That is, if money is allocated to a firm in industry A then we need to bear in mind that the same money cannot also be allocated to a firm in industry B. So, when judging, say, a 10% rate of return from

the first company, we compare it with the next best alternative use, in this case industry B (assuming the same risk in A and B). If the firm in industry B is expected to generate 9% per year then by investing in A rather than B, we create value. If alternatives are estimated in a variety of companies and sectors then the return on capital can be increased because of the greater range of options.

Investment 18

BUFFETT'S INVESTMENT IN SANITY

While Warren Buffett was busily adding subsidiaries to Berkshire Hathaway in 1969, he was increasingly anxious about the attitude of other share buyers. This attitude was exemplified by a statement made by an investment manager at one of the leading mutual funds when launching a new advisory service:

> "The complexities of national and international economics make money management a full-time job. A good money manager cannot maintain a study of securities on a week-by-week or even a day-by-day basis. Securities must be studied in a minute-by-minute program."[71]

To which Buffett's response, in typical jokey fashion but with a hard intellectual edge, was:

> "Wow! This sort of stuff makes me feel guilty when I go out for a Pepsi. When practiced by large and increasing numbers of highly motivated people with huge amounts of money on a limited quantity of suitable securities, the result becomes highly unpredictable. In some ways it is fascinating to watch and in other ways it is appalling."[72]

Buffett had learned from Graham, and had himself repeatedly preached the following:

- Investment is about understanding the business, for which you need to conduct thorough analysis.

- Short-term, or even medium-term, movements of shares on a stock market are usually unrelated and irrelevant to what is happening at the coalface of your business. In the long run the market will recognise intrinsic value, but for many months (or years) in between you can be sure that the market will do some very odd things.

This message is as relevant today as it was in 1969.

Nothing to buy

Buffett went on to say that, sticking to his investment principles, he was finding it very difficult to find companies worth investing in:

> "I can't emphasize too strongly that the quality and quantity of ideas is presently at an all time low... Sometimes I feel we should have a plaque in our office like the one at the headquarters of Texas Instruments in Dallas which reads: 'We don't believe in miracles, we rely on them.' It is possible for an old, overweight ball player, whose legs and batting eye are gone, to tag a fast ball on the nose for a pinch-hit home run, but you don't change your line-up because of it. We have a number of important negatives operating on our future and, while they shouldn't add up to futility, they certainly don't add up to more than an average of quite moderate profitability."[73]

There is also a positive message from this: if you stick to sound investment principles you stop yourself investing any money at times when there are no bargains to be found – your investment fund can thereby accumulate as cash. Then, when bargains are more plentiful, you allow yourself to invest again. This method provides some immunity from market mood infection.

Low costs

Also around this time, Buffett made some comments on frugality, or whether a big research team was needed to be a successful fund manager: "On January 1, 1962 we consolidated the predecessor limited partnerships, moved out of the bedroom and hired our first full-time employees. Net assets at that time were $7,178,500. From that point to our present net assets of $104,429,431 we have added one person to the payroll."[74]

Buffett decided to retire

Buffett finally got so irritated with the investment environment that he announced his retirement, aged 38. At the end of May 1969 he sent a letter that stunned his partners.

Buffett had contemplated both the disturbing mood that the share market had got itself into and the personal cost of continuing to pour his whole being into share analysis to the exclusion of family life.

When he had first mentioned his need to change direction 18 months previously, he denied that he wanted to quit, but he had said that he wanted to ease-back so that he had more time for family and other interests, and put more effort into building controlled companies over a long time frame, working with people he liked, trusted and admired. Buffett wanted the pleasure of building those relationships, even if that meant lowering expectations in terms of annual returns on capital.

For that 18 months, the great majority of partners were of the view that Buffett should continue – even with the lowered return expectations the likelihood was that he would still be an excellent manager of money. But by May 1969 Buffett had decided he wanted to end the partnership soon.

The market was no longer conducive

First, Buffett explained his frustration with the market:

"(1) Opportunities for investment that are open to the analyst who stresses quantitative factors have virtually disappeared, after rather steadily drying up over the past twenty years;

(2) Our $100 million of assets further eliminates a large portion of this seemingly barren investment world, since commitments of less than about $3 million cannot have a real impact on our overall performance, and this virtually rules out companies with less than about $100 million of common stock at market value; and

(3) A swelling interest in investment performance has created an increasingly short-term oriented and (in my opinion) more speculative market."[75]

Even when Buffett did find bargains (particularly net current asset value bargains), they would often be very small companies that he could not invest in, because he would have to take an inconveniently large proportion of the issued shares to have a meaningful impact on the portfolio.

Buffett was fed up with the fashion for short-term performance measurement relative to the market. He did not want the hassle of trying to compete with the short-termists when his preference was to build up companies.

The personal reasons

With a sigh, Buffett noted that he had earlier expressed recognition of his need to gear-down his 100% focus on the partnership. However, in trying to do so it became very clear that his psychological make-up caused him to be congenitally incapable of a slower pace – he could not bear to let people down and he liked to be the best at what he did:

"I have flunked this test completely during the last eighteen months… As long as I am 'on stage', publishing a regular record and assuming responsibility for management of what amounts to virtually 100% of the net worth of many partners, I will never be able to put sustained effort into any non-BPL activity… I know I don't want to be totally occupied with out-pacing an investment rabbit all my life. The only way to slow down is to stop."[76]

Then he revealed the bombshell: "Therefore, before yearend, I intend to give all limited partners the required formal notice of my intention to retire."[77]

Partners were offered alternative homes for their money

Buffett did not want to simply abandon his partners in 1969. He had a powerful sense of responsibility. He considered recommendations on where they should put the money they were about to receive from him, if they did not want to invest it for themselves. His thinking was guided by these objectives:

- **To suggest an alternative fund manager.** This person must have both integrity and ability. He/she "will probably perform as well or better than I would in the future (although nowhere close to what he or I have achieved in the past)."[78] This was not immodesty – Buffett thought he could never again achieve what he had in the past. A further criterion was that the manager would welcome even small sums and thus would accept even the partners of limited means.

- **Partners would have the option to receive cash and/or marketable securities** of those companies "where I like both the prospects and price but which partners will be able to freely convert to cash if they wish."[79]

- **The possibility of maintaining proportional holdings in Berkshire Hathaway and Diversified Retailing.** Partners were warned that these two shareholdings were "not freely marketable (various SEC restrictions apply to 'control' stock and non-registered stock) and they will probably be both non-transferable and non-income-producing for a considerable period of time."[80]

A big decision

Fundamentally, Buffett wanted his partners to be free to either take cash or shares in one or both small companies where there were downsides of both poor/no liquidity and no dividends. What would you do?

Of course, with hindsight we'd all invest in Berkshire Hathaway and become millionaires from our initial holding of a thousand dollars. But, at that time, BH consisted of a failing textile business, a small Omaha insurance business that was making returns on capital of about 20% per year, a small bank making good returns, a tiny newspaper and a couple of even smaller businesses. Diversified Retail was not diversified at all – it was a chain of retail stores selling cheap stuff, mostly in run-down areas of towns. Back then, it was not a clear-cut decision.

For many partners however, the factor that swung their decision was the offer of Buffett's continuing involvement with both BH and Diversified Retail (DR). They backed the person, even though evidence to date of BH's and DR's success was limited. Buffett made plain what he thought of the companies (note the emphasis on people and relationships):

> "I strongly like all of the people running our controlled businesses (joined now by the Illinois National Bank and Trust Company of Rockford, Illinois, a $100 million plus, extremely well-run bank, purchased by Berkshire Hathaway earlier this year), and want the relationship to be life long. I certainly have no desire to sell a good controlled business run by people I like and admire, merely to obtain a fancy

price. However, specific conditions may cause the sale of one operating unit at some point."[81]

Buffett wanted to go out with a bang

Buffett said that he had one final objective for the partnership, "to go out with a bang". However, he fully expected that this would not happen and that 1969 would be a poor year. His best guess was that "we will show a breakeven result for 1969 before any monthly payments to partners."[82]

Buffett admitted that he would have postponed liquidating the partnership for a year or two if the stock market had been more conducive to finding gems: "Quite frankly, in spite of any factors set forth on the earlier pages. I would continue to operate the Partnership in 1970, or even 1971, if I had some really first class ideas. Not because I want to, but simply because I would so much rather end with a good year than a poor one. However. I just don't see anything available that gives any reasonable hope of delivering such a good year and I have no desire to grope around, hoping to 'get lucky' with other people's money. I am not attuned to this market environment and I don't want to spoil a decent record by trying to play a game I don't understand just so I can go out a hero. Therefore, we will be liquidating holdings throughout the year."[83]

Bill Ruane was recommended as a fund manager

Buffett was pretty consistent in producing returns for his partners. But the person he recommended as a first-class fund manager, Bill Ruane, had shown a 50% fall in his client's funds in 1962. In 1963 he only just broke even. In the nine months to October 1969, when Buffett recommended Ruane in a letter to partners, he had lost about 15%. I find this little piece of investing history very encouraging. Buffett still regarded Ruane as the best, despite short-term underperformance.

The key question is: why? What was Buffett looking at when he judged Ruane to be excellent? First, there was the overall performance. From 1956 to 1961 and from 1964 to 1968, the return on a composite of Ruane's individual client accounts averaged over 40% per annum. That was better than Buffett had achieved. More important was the soundness of the principles Ruane followed.

Bill Ruane the investor

Ruane graduated from Harvard Business School in 1949. From there he followed the well-trodden path of Ivy Leaguers to Wall Street. But then, as Buffett put it in his great talk, 'The Superinvestors at Graham-and-Doddsville' (given at Columbia University in 1984[84]), "he realised that he needed to get a real business education so he came up to take Ben [Graham's] course at Columbia." This is where the 21-year-old Buffett met Ruane in 1951. Buffett therefore knew Ruane's intellectual origins.

Buffett regarded Ruane as a true investor and said that he "ranks the highest when combining the factors of integrity, ability and continued availability to all partners."[85] In the letter he continued appraising his personality: "I have had considerable opportunity to observe his qualities of character, temperament and intellect since that time. If Susie and I were to die while our children are minors, he is one of three trustees who have *carte blanche* on investment matters."[86]

A logical caveat

Buffett is so rational and honest that he would not let this character reference stand without qualifying it with the possibility, however small, that he was wrong:

> "There is no way to eliminate the possibility of error when judging humans particularly in regard to future behavior in an unknown environment. However, decisions have to be made – whether actively or passively – and I consider Bill to be an exceptionally high probability decision on character and a high probability one on investment performance. I also consider it likely that Bill will continue as a money manager for many years to come."[87]

Did the investors from Graham-and-Doddsville tend to hold the same shares?

Buffett noted that Ruane's investment style, despite the common Graham-Dodd origins, was different from his. There were very few securities they both held at the same time.

Indeed, in the Columbia talk Buffett highlighted the performances of eight value investors that had been touched through direct learning from Graham, but which tended to hold completely different portfolios. Furthermore, they each held to different styles of value investing, with say Walter Schloss (one of the four *peasants* at Graham-Newman in 1954, meaning an analyst who was not a partner) focused on quantitative data and investing in a widely diversified portfolio (over 100 investments), while Charlie Munger in California held a concentrated portfolio of excellent economic franchise shares with little emphasis on the balance sheet.

There were many common threads of the Graham and Dodd investors though, for instance:

1. Analyse the business rather than the stock market movements.

2. Build in a margin of safety.

3. Look for reasonable returns only.

4. Understand and exploit Mr Market's moods rather than participate in them.

Bill Ruane had previously worked with only small sums

Until the point of Buffett's recommendation, Ruane had been working with about $5m to $10m, but by 1969 it rose from $20m to $30m. It did worry Buffett that Ruane might encounter problems if he was to take on a much larger sum:

- Sheer size "will tend to moderate performance".[88] There would be fewer bargains to choose from given the raised minimum market capitalisation required.

- He could get bogged down in the detail of running the business operation of managing a fund rather than spending all his time thinking about investments.

- If he was good there was a high probability "that even excellent investment management during the next decade will only produce limited advantages over passive management"[89] due to the strange market period in which he had to operate.

Despite these negatives, Buffett said they were "not the sort of drawbacks leading to horrible performance, but more likely the sort of things that lead to average performance. I think this is the main risk you run with Bill – and average performance is just not that terrible a risk."[90] Ruane set up the Sequoia Fund to handle the money coming from Buffett's partners.

Buffett's partnership breakup

In late November 1969, Buffett formally gave 30 days' notice of his intent to retire from the partnership. In an earlier letter he had expressed his expectation that each partner would receive a cash payment amounting to about 56% of their start of the year share of the partnership. But, because he sold securities for more than anticipated, the figure ended up at 64% in January 1970.

In addition, they would get proportional shareholdings in Diversified Retailing and Berkshire Hathaway. However, if they chose to dispose of these shares, then that would bring more cash amounting to 30% to 35% of their 1 January 1969 capital. That still left some capital tied up in securities. Buffett expected to sell these in the first half of 1970. Thus further cash payments were to be expected. Quite rationally, Buffett did not want to rush the process and so allowed for the possibility that even after June 1970 securities might still remain to be liquidated and a final distribution made.

The two companies

At the end of 1969, the Buffett Partnership owned:

- 800,000 of the 1,000,000 shares in Diversified Retailing Company. Diversified Retailing owned 100% of Associated Retail Stores.

- 691,441 of the 983,582 (70%) shares in Berkshire Hathaway.

Buffett did not want to oversell the attractions of holding shares in these two companies, but did let his partners know that he was going to put the bulk of his wealth into them and he believed their prospects were good.

An end to partner-like fiduciary duty?

Buffett bluntly declared that the technical relationship between him and his partners was about to change. For those who held on to DRC and BH shares, Buffett would merely be a fellow shareholder and a director. He would no longer have the moral or legal responsibilities of being a managing partner. It was all very well Buffett stating this, but as we have already seen it was not in his make-up to set aside his sense of stewardship, or paternalism.

If you know anything about Warren Buffett, and certainly if you have met him, you know that he treats shareholders as though they are partners. He welcomes all BH shareholders to Omaha and tries his best to keep them informed about the company. And he provides his managerial and investment services for virtually nothing.

But back then he was trying to shift the weight of responsibility off his shoulders. He said in his letter of 5 December 1969 that he did not want the obligation of always holding these shares, nor to always be committing his time to them:

> "I want to stress that I will not be in a managerial or partnership status with you regarding your future holdings of such securities. You will be free to do what you wish with your stock in the future and so, of course, will I. I think that there is a very high probability that I will maintain my investment in DRC and BH for a very long period, but I want no implied moral commitment to do so nor do I wish to advise others over an indefinite future period regarding their holdings. The companies, of course, will keep all shareholders advised of their activities and you will receive reports as issued by them, probably on a semi-annual basis. Should I continue to hold the securities, as I fully expect to do, my degree of involvement in their activities may vary depending upon my other interests. The odds are that I will take an important position on matters of policy, but I want no moral obligation to be other than a passive shareholder, should my interests develop elsewhere."[91]

Learning points

1. **Market moods can be incomprehensible to value investors.** Caution is needed at such times.

2. **High cash balances are a suitable policy within an investment portfolio when few investments are available with a good margin of safety.**

3. **Behave with integrity and diligence toward those who you partner in business.**

4. **Short-term (a year or so) performance statistics are meaningless in judging investment ability.** If sound principles are adopted, performance will follow.

5. **Small investors have an advantage.** They can invest in companies with small market capitalisations, thus widening the range of available investees.

Investment 19

BLUE CHIP STAMPS

Summary of the deal

Deal	Blue Chip Stamps
Time	1968–present
Price paid	$3m–$4m (initially)
Quantity	7.5% of the company's shares (initially)
Sale price	Absorbed in Berkshire Hathaway
Profit	Hundreds of millions of dollars

Towards the end of 1969, the Buffett Partnership held a substantial stake in Blue Chip Stamps (BCS) worth about 6% of the fund. This stake had been built up, starting in 1968, when the market capitalisation of BCS was around $40m. Charlie Munger, along with his friend and fellow Benjamin Graham student, Rick Guerin, had also spotted the opportunity in Blue Chip Stamps, and had also bought shares.

Alongside other holdings, Buffett tried to sell the 371,400 BCS shares owned by the partnership (7.5% of the total BCS shares) so he could hand the cash to his partners. He thought he had a deal at about $24. Then the stock market fell and the buyer wanted a much lower price, and then a lower price still.

In the end, a small amount of shares were sold elsewhere, but the bulk were retained until Buffett could find a "more advantageous disposal or eventual distribution to our partners... even if it takes a year or two."[92] As it turned out, this forced hold became very profitable.

Let's backtrack a moment to find out how the Buffett Partnership came to be invested in BCS in the first place.

The stamps business

During the late 1960s and early 1970s, it was fashionable to collect stamps from retailers. When you bought something, along with your change you got dozens of stamps – petrol stations handed out a lot of them. You took the stamps home and stuck them in a book, many pages long. The books of stamps could be swapped for toasters, kettles, tables, etc. The beauty of the business was that BCS received a fee – cash upfront – from retailers for the stamps. The cash was used later to buy the toasters, etc.

Significantly, between the time when retailers paid for the stamps and the point the stamps were redeemed by customers, there was a big pile of cash – a float – sitting in BCS. Which other Buffett business does that remind you of? Of course it's insurance, where people part with their cash long before claims are paid. On top of the float, BCS got a boost when people did not redeem the stamps when they were lost, when there were too few to redeem, or when the stamps were simply forgotten about.

About $120m of BCS stamps were sold to retailers each year and the float was in the region of $60m–$100m.

Why were Blue Chip Stamps shares cheap in the late 1960s?

BCS was founded by nine large retail groups in 1956. These companies, including gasoline stations, handed out the stamps. Other retail stores could also offer the stamps, but had no say in how the business was run, nor could they share in the profits. These small retailers knew that BCS could exploit them, so they went to the antitrust authorities, and in 1967 obtained a complete reorganisation of the company.

As a result, many more shares had to be created, amounting to 55% of the company, and these were offered to the smaller retailers. Those shares not sold to retailers could be unloaded on the market.

Thousands of small retailers ended up with shares they did not really want and thus the price fell. Buffett, Munger and Guerin bought aggressively at that time.

Buffett reflected on Blue Chip business in his 2006 BH letter:

> "Every now and then Charlie and I catch on early to a tide-like trend, one brimming over with commercial promise... the two of us jumped into the reward business way back in 1970 by buying control of a trading stamp operation, Blue Chip Stamps. In that year, Blue Chip had sales of $126 million, and its stamps papered California. In 1970, indeed, about 60 billion of our stamps were licked by savers, pasted into books, and taken to Blue Chip redemption stores. Our catalog of rewards was 116 pages thick and chock full of tantalizing items... I was told that even certain brothels and mortuaries gave stamps to their patrons."[93]

Buffett and Munger eventually advanced to the BCS board and took over the investment committee. With that, Buffett had another large pot of money to play with.

An example of Buffett's use of Blue Chip Stamps' money

One of the businesses in which BCS invested was See's Candies, in 1973. It is still owned by BH today. It was bought for $25m in 1973 and has generated over $1.9bn in pre-tax earnings while only using an additional $40m in investment capital. This exciting story is recounted in the next chapter (Investment 20).

Learning points

1. **Float is a very useful way to leverage a skilled investor's resources to gain additional returns, supplying interest-free funds.** Float (money held in reserve available for investment for a period) is available in many types of business, not just insurance. For example, trading stamps, Christmas hamper clubs and some holiday companies.

2. **A buying opportunity may arise when there are many reluctant holders of shares.** The price could be pushed down if many shareholders are not especially committed to the company.

3. **A failing operating business does not necessarily make for a bad investment** if the resources can be redirected to generate superior rates of return.

4. **Working with like-minded investors can allow greater influence and therefore a better outcome for all shareholders.** Through cooperation Buffett, Munger and Guerin were able to dominate BCS and thereby change the sources of its income for the better.

Investment 20

SEE'S CANDIES

Summary of the deal

Deal	See's Candies
Time	1972–present
Price paid	$25m
Quantity	All the company's shares
Sale price	Still part of Berkshire Hathaway
Profit	$2bn and counting

The 39-year-old Buffett had been running investments for partners for more than 13 years, and the partners had received a compound annual return of 23.8%. This was after Buffett had taken his fees for managing the fund. Before fees, the return was an astonishing 29.5% per year, compared with the return on the Dow Jones of around 8% per year in the same period. An investor who put $10,000 into Buffett's Partnership in 1957 could have about $160,000 in 1970.

In 1969, at the point the partnership was about to be dissolved, there were 99 partners. Some wanted to take all of their cash from the partnership and sold their allocated shares in Berkshire

Hathaway and Diversified Retailing. They had received 64% of their value in the partnership in cash and most of the rest as shares in these two companies. The rump partnership fund held 371,400 shares in Blue Chip Stamps (7.5% of the company), which Buffett expected to sell soon, and then direct the money to the partners.

Many partners, aware that their friend Buffett was going to take major shareholdings in Berkshire Hathaway and Diversified Retailing, decided to go along for the ride, keeping at least some of their shares in those two companies. This was in spite of the fact that Buffett had said the shares would have no/little liquidity and offer no dividends. But the prevailing attitude was: if they were good enough for Buffett, they were good enough for them. If Buffett was buying, that was all you needed to know.

Buffett's quarter-share of the partnership fund meant that he was very wealthy indeed; he had come a long way from the boy scrabbling around for a few cents. One option was to retire and live a life of idleness and luxury. But this did not appeal to him. He loved the fun of business, the intellectual challenge of the game, the ongoing painting on a great canvas.

While he did turn to other things, such as overseeing the Buffett Foundation which granted 50 scholarships per year for black college students, he remained devoted to business. The emphasis was now most definitely on those businesses controlled by Buffett with his large percentage holdings.

The daily routine

The Buffett empire was controlled from a small office in Kiewit Plaza, a few blocks from his Omaha home. Typically his 8.30am to 5pm office day was mostly spent making phone calls (including regular calls with Charlie Munger) or simply reading. He had only four or five assistants at this head office who covered the mundane tasks such as dealing with stockbrokers, keeping accounts and correspondence.

Committing to his companies

Buffett decided to put the bulk of his wealth into Berkshire Hathaway. He quickly added to the pile of Berkshire Hathaway shares he received from the partnership fund to build the stake controlled by him and his wife Susie to around 29% by late spring 1970. The shares were then trading at around $43. Thus his holding had a market value of approximately $12m.

He also built up his portion of Diversified Retailing to about 40% of the 1m shares. These were worth perhaps $12 each (based on tangible net assets), so he held about $5m here.

Also on his desk was the problem of Blue Chip Stamps. Having failed to sell the shares in 1969 they were languishing, waiting for a new home. He decided to hold on to some of these for himself. At first this was a small single digit percentage of the shares, but by the end of the year he was into double digits.

If he had wanted to, Buffett could have put his hands behind his head, tipped back in his chair and thought contented thoughts about the wonderful machinery producing profits for him: Ken Chace was running the textile business, Eugene Abegg was running Illinois National Bank, Jack Ringwalt was running National Indemnity, Ben Rosner was running Associated Retail Stores, and he had key people he could trust running some smaller businesses. Buffett could read the monthly financial data sent by these excellent managers and watch the money flowing in.

But no, these businesses were generating surplus cash that could be deployed elsewhere. That is very tempting – a flow of cash to invest! And they each had floats of one sort or another. Buffett had to allocate all this money well and he wanted the fun of finding new gems.

Buffett's three holdings with potential in 1970

1. Berkshire Hathaway

With 29% of the votes at Berkshire Hathaway, plus the loyalty of other shareholders, many of whom were former partners, Buffett could dominate the boardroom and capital allocation decisions. BH had morphed from being a textiles-only company in the mid-1960s with $22m of tangible net assets, to a mini-conglomerate with about $50m of tangible assets. This money was split roughly equally between three distinct businesses:

1. A textile operation that earned very little, if anything – 1969 was one of the better years with a 5% return on capital employed.

2. Illinois National Bank (Rockford Bank), which had recently been bought.

3. An insurance business. This had branched out from automobile insurance into workmen's compensation and reinsurance. Most significant for Buffett was the combination of managers capable of making a positive return on underwriting and a float of $39m, which he could invest.

There was another $2m of Berkshire's money invested in miscellaneous assets. The $7m of debt taken on to buy the Rockford Bank had to be deducted to arrive at net tangible assets of $43m, which was about the same as BH's market capitalisation. For the sake of completeness, I should mention that BH held the *Omaha Sun* and Blacker Printing Company, but they were very small and did not feature much in the future of the holding company.

Overall, BH made a return of more than 10% on average stockholders' equity in 1969, with the combined bank and insurance operations producing rates of return in the low teens.

When expressed separately, Buffett had said in 1969 that National Indemnity was earning about 20% on capital employed.

Buffett reckoned that the earnings power (forward-looking, but based partly on evidence from the past) of the bank and insurance together was about $4m. On the $32m invested in these tangible assets, a $4m cash inflow indicates a return on capital of around 12.5%.

Would you invest in Berkshire Hathaway in 1970?

I think you would agree that these numbers are OK, but they are hardly astounding; they hardly indicated that Berkshire Hathaway would one day be a top four company in the US. In fact, if I was transported back in time to 1970 and was asked to analyse Berkshire Hathaway I might conclude that, while it had a great captain, the business operations were pretty mundane, and it had overall failed to prove an ability to generate high rates of return on capital employed. It is no surprise that the share price had risen no higher than the book value per share.

It would be hard to take any impression other than the business did not point to exciting future growth.

Perhaps, if I was having a really exceptionally perceptive day, I might have noted that Berkshire had a flow of profits from the bank which could be invested elsewhere, an insurance float of $39m, and also dribs and drabs coming from reduced textile operations and insurance underwriting profits. Thus, month-by-month, Buffett would have some cash to play with. And it could get even better if he got hold of more insurance companies with more float.

Admittedly, the vast majority of the insurance float had to be kept in very safe investments, that is Treasury bills and bonds, rather than shares, as a back-up for insurance claims, but that still left a proportion to be placed in the stock market where Buffett could work his usual magic. But this was not as great as it sounds, at least for the immediate future, because Buffett was not active in the stock market in 1970, as he was unable to find bargains.

Making a sober assessment, I would have probably looked at the business Buffett was getting into, that was buoyed only with a pathetic textile operation, a newly-acquired bank with an elderly patriarch wanting to retire, and a small insurance operation, and have concluded that however hard Buffett rowed, this boat was not going to get very far. Buffett said himself that he was only expecting the $4m figure of owner earnings to grow at a rate of 10% per annum. This would be hardly a great rate considering that, if no dividends were paid, tangible net assets would increase at about the same pace.

Acknowledging the mediocre business background of Berkshire Hathaway in 1970 reinforces the point that the Buffett story is not one of inevitable progress, or one of un-deflectable glorious destiny. At many times in his career, Buffett found himself with blunt tools and unpromising shapeless materials. It was up to him to turn them into something beautiful.

2. Diversified Retailing Company

The second holding with potential was Diversified Retailing Company. Buffett built up a 40% stake in a chain of 80 dress shops in early 1970 – Associated Cotton Shops, renamed Associated Retail Stores – which produced after-tax profits of around $1m. This was a return of around 20% on the capital employed.

DRC had recently sold Hochschild-Kohn, for which it received $5.045m in cash from Supermarkets General. Furthermore, as additional payment, DRC held debt in Supermarkets General, $2m of which was due for repayment in early 1970 and $4.54m was due in early 1971. Thus Buffett could expect over $11m of cash to accumulate over the following few months. So here was another pot of money to be used for investments; when companies and shares were selling at bargain prices again, he'd be ready to strike.

3. Blue Chip Stamps

The third holding with potential, Blue Chip Stamps, was just a nuisance. The trading stamps business was dying so there was no value to be had in the operational side there. Buffett had stated his intention in his 31 December 1969 letter to partners: "advantageous disposal or eventual distribution to our partners". But he seemed to have second thoughts. Here was yet another pot of money for him to invest. Blue Chip Stamps' float was even bigger than Berkshire's, at somewhere between $60m and $100m, and Buffett and Munger were in charge of the investment committee.

An exciting future lay ahead

So, from an operating business point of view, we see an unprepossessing start to Buffett's new career as a controller of a group of small companies. The way in which he played the hand he was dealt is a fascinating story, containing many lessons for how to allocate capital, motivate people and select shares.

What would Buffett do in the next two years?

There were two, perhaps opposing, forces on Buffett at the start of this new phase in his life. First, the operating companies were (generally) throwing-off cash. In 1970 this was about $5m post-tax, split between roughly $4m coming from BH and $1m from DRC. But look at this growth: by 1972 the operating earnings of BH alone were $11.1m. The second force was that Buffett could not invest much of the money in shares because he could not find many bargains.

Buffett had excellent people looking after his businesses who understood his requirement to generate satisfactory rates of return on each additional dollar invested; if the next dollar could not get sufficient return in that business, then it should be handed over to Buffett to be invested elsewhere. To recap, these were the excellent managers at the businesses:

Jack Ringwalt, 66, was doing a great job at National Indemnity, generating double-digit percentage returns and growing the profitable underwriting business for BH. Reinsurance had grown to be a substantial business by 1972. Small insurance companies were acquired.

Eugene Abegg, 73, at Illinois National Bank really knew how to produce return on capital for BH.

Ken Chace, 55, was overseeing the survival of the Berkshire Hathaway textile business and cutting down on the capital used, so that it shrank to under one-fifth of BH's net assets.

Ben Rosner, 70, at Diversified Retail's Associated Retail Stores, was getting over 20% return on net tangible assets.

As well as the operating business cash surplus, Buffett could look to the floats he controlled: the insurance float rose to $69.5m in 1972; Diversified Retail had around $11m in cash in early 1971, and Blue Chip Stamps had $60m–$100m.

So there were at least three different pots of money he could draw from for future investment adventures. Each pot had a different set of minority shareholders with a claim on the value within their pot. Buffett thought of these shareholders as loyal and trusting partners, sharing his values, and to be treated with absolute decency and fairness.

Let's now look at one of the uses to which Buffett put the cash at his disposal – his investment in See's Candies.

See's Candies – before the deal

Mrs See

Mrs See is a character used by See's in their marketing – a genuine old photo placed on the boxes – but there really was a Mrs See. Mary was the widowed mother of Charles A. See. Mother, son and daughter-in-law, Florence, together began making candy for sale from their Pasadena bungalow in 1921. They quickly earned a reputation for their high-quality, old-style candy. Over the next few years they opened stores throughout California and became a much-loved institution; people grew up eating See's Candies as a treat. In 1949, Laurence, Charles's son, took over an operation with 78 stores. Laurence's brother, Charles B. 'Harry' See also worked for the company.

Chuck Huggins

Chuck Huggins was to become Buffett's key man at See's, producing about $2bn in cash for Buffett to invest in other companies, so it is useful to have some brief background to his story. Born in 1925, he was a paratrooper in the second world war and later studied English. After a dead-end salesman job he was interviewed by Laurence See and hired in 1951. Initially Huggins worked for the general manager and was asked to do a great variety of tasks. His talent led to rapid promotion. In 1969, Laurence See died at 57, and his brother Harry was not willing to carry on running the firm – it was said he wanted to enjoy "wine and girls" instead. Chuck Huggins, now vice president of the 150-shop enterprise, was asked to find a buyer.

Blue Chip Stamps' interest

An investment advisor to Blue Chip Stamps, Robert Flaherty, discovered that See's was up for sale in 1971. He and William Ramsey, a Blue Chip Stamps executive, telephoned Buffett expressing their keenness to buy it. Buffett's first reaction was that he did not want to be in the candy business, thinking that the companies were expensive. Then the phone went dead.

By the time Flaherty and Ramsey were reconnected, Buffett had looked at See's accounts, and he had softened his line: he would be willing to buy it – at a price. Towards the end of November

1971, Warren Buffett, Charlie Munger and Rick Guerin went to a Los Angeles hotel room to meet Harry See and Chuck Huggins, the latter two having no idea who these investors were, other than that they ran some small investment organisations.

Munger, the Californian, was very familiar with See's and its quality reputation in that state. The brand was so strong that would-be competitors needed to spend a fortune to take significant market share from them, should they ever try. There was intense brand loyalty to See's, bordering on fanaticism.

After some time, Buffett said he would be interested in buying the company but first he needed to know who would be running it afterwards. Buffett made plain that he had no one on his side that could take on the role. Harry See responded that Huggins would be the person for the job. The three representatives from Blue Chip asked if Huggins would meet them the next day, which he did. During three hours of questioning at that second meeting Huggins was disarmingly honest about the negative aspects of the business as well as its virtues.

Huggins figured that such smart guys would discover the negatives anyway and so it was best to acknowledge them up front. Besides, Huggins would be working for them afterwards if the deal went through, so it was best to build the relationship on an honest base. His integrity, realism and rationality greatly impressed Buffett, Munger and Guerin.

For his part, Huggins was also impressed. Buffett asked astute questions and focused on the core business issues. He was reassured that he would be working with remarkably clever and business-interested bosses, who also placed great emphasis on decency and honour. For example, they wanted Huggins to maintain the high ethics the See's family had instilled in the business culture, keep enhancing the reputation of the brand and offer the highest standards of service.

They wanted him to keep running it the way it had been run up until now – after all, he knew more about the operations, employees and customers than they did. Their role might be to look after the business in the long run, making sure it had adequate capital backing, encouraging its values and helping to broaden the horizons of its senior managers.

Huggins was so impressed by Buffett, Munger and Guerin that he was fired with enthusiasm to do all he could to assist the development of the business should Blue Chip end up taking it over. But, it was far from certain that Blue Chip would do so.

The deal

Buffett and Munger were hesitant to buy in November 1971. After all, net tangible assets were only $8m and after-tax profits were about $2m. Thus the asking price of $30m seemed high to them from both the balance sheet perspective and the earnings perspective. Ira Marshall (Munger's partner at the investment fund Wheeler, Munger and Co.) helped to convince them that this was a special company and worth paying more for, with Munger wading in to persuade Buffett. There was one great positive element in the above numbers: a 25% after-tax return on net tangible assets.

Also, See's at that time was selling candy at about the same price as a major competitor, Russell Stover, but the Blue Chip Stamps team thought that it had untapped pricing power and could, over time, charge an increasing premium over Russell Stover. They figured if Blue Chip paid $25m, then with a post-tax profit of $2m that would be an 8% earnings yield even without raising prices (the 10-year Treasury rate in November 1971 was 5.8%).

But if earnings could be put on a fast-rising trend through the leverage of what Buffett became increasingly convinced was "uncapped pricing power", it wouldn't be long before earnings rose from about $4m pre-tax to $6.5m–$7m. That would occur with a price rise of just another 15c on each pound (compared with the then $1.85).

Given Buffett's adherence to Benjamin Graham's principles, it was quite a leap for him to be willing to buy a business at more than three times net tangible asset value, let alone an even higher multiple of net current asset value. He was allowing his boundaries to be pushed by Munger and others, towards including companies with excellent business franchises that he regarded as being within his circle of competence.

Despite his shift, Buffett and Munger set a strict limit of $25m — they were prepared to walk away from the deal if any more was asked. That was quite a distance from what Harry See was looking for. Finally, Harry agreed to $25m so that he could get on with his life, and the deal was finally completed on 3 January 1972, with Blue Chip Stamps buying 99% of the company. The other 1% was acquired in 1978.

After the purchase

As soon as the purchase was agreed, Huggins (who was made President and CEO) and Buffett arranged a very simple remuneration package. It was discussed for a mere five minutes, never written on paper and lasted for decades.

Buffett, true to nature, started to take a keen interest in some of the key aspects of the business, particularly things to do with finance, such as sugar and cocoa futures. Huggins was not required to regularly meet Buffett or anyone else from Blue Chip or Berkshire. However, data were something that Buffett looked forward to receiving, so he got sales and other statistics frequently. But note, his need for data was not so that he could direct Huggins in how to sell more candy or improve the business; he just took an interest in the performance, particularly return on capital employed.

While Buffett did not regularly phone Huggins or look over his shoulder, he was available to consult should Huggins need to talk something over. He could call Buffett whenever he liked and Buffett would answer, or, if he was unable to do so, would call him back within an hour.

Both sides felt the relationship was more friend and confidant, partner and equal, rather than boss and employee. Buffett never ordered Huggins to do anything, but helped to examine the options when decisions had to be made. Drawing on his deep and wide knowledge of business success and failure, Buffett might have a few options Huggins had not seen — but he would not insist, merely ask if the decision-maker, Huggins, might like to consider this or that.

The franchise

See's never diverged from its chosen path of building a business franchise around quality candy. It didn't make sense to change the business in any fundamental way, nor to diversify. Candy making and selling is what it knew, and in those areas See's had a durable competitive advantage. Why dilute managerial effort by doing other things, or expand to places where that vital quality of reputation was not in the minds of the candy-buying public?

Buffett and Huggins agreed on the need to keep building the franchise, deepening and widening the business' moat, by never compromising on the quality of the product, using only the best ingredients, with no preservatives, and never compromising on customer service, even if that meant a short-term profit hit.

Buffett has said that investors never stop learning and he is still learning himself, even after being taught by Benjamin Graham and decades of experience. The See's business was a great educator; it rammed home the importance of the affection with which a brand can be held in people's minds (Buffett refers to *mind share*, rather than *market share*). This can provide a basis for price rises and exceptional returns on capital employed.

This idea led to even more valuable decisions later. As Buffett put it, "It's one thing to own stock in Coca-Cola or something, but when you're actually in the business of making determinations about opening stores and pricing decisions, you learn from it. We have made a lot more money out of See's than shows from the earnings of See's, just by the fact that it's educated me, and I'm sure it's educated Charlie too."[94]

Expansion attempts

In 1972, there were 167 See's stores. Every now and then the managerial team, and Buffett and Munger, wondered if they were missing potential good profits (good meaning high relative to equity capital devoted) by not expanding outside of the western states, and California in particular.

Thus they devoted very limited amounts of capital to test the See's model elsewhere. For example, in the late 1980s they opened stores in Colorado, Missouri and Texas. But this experiment did not work due to poor preparation in terms of brand recognition and so the company withdrew. The people in these other states were not willing to pay a premium for an unfamiliar brand of candy. Thus there were still only slightly over 200 stores in the 1980s, similar to the number today.

One expansion attempt, however, was a great success. Buffett pretends to be an old man who doesn't understand new technology and avoids computers and the internet. In reality, he has a very good grasp of the potential of new technology. Thus, the person who pushed in 1998 for an internet sales strategy was Buffett – this is now a significant source of revenue and growth for See's.

We have seen before that Buffett loves to keep hold of able and seasoned managers. He managed to persuade Huggins to keep working until he was 81 years of age. On his retirement, Huggins could look back on 54 years with the company, and 33 as CEO.

In 2006, Brad Kinstler, who had worked with Buffett for decades in the insurance business, was asked to take over See's. The fundamentals of the business have not changed much under Kinstler. Even in 2012, all of the 211 shops were west of Chicago, of which 110 were in California. See's went where customers had an affection for their particular candy and were willing to pay a premium for it. See's also opened kiosks at airports. Since 2012, new outlets have been opened in eastern states. But the expansion is measured. First, they went for seasonal carts in shopping malls. In those few towns where significant demand was found a store might have opened, but even then risk is limited by only spending around $300,000 per unit.

Pricing power

Discussions about pricing

Buffett worked with Huggins to set candy prices annually. He felt it was important that a person with a wider perspective and greater financial interest should have input on the pricing process. He felt that a manager may be averse to raising prices, because:

"The manager has just one business. His equation tells him that if he prices too low, it's not that serious. But if he prices too high, he sees himself screwing up the only thing in his life. And no one knows what raising prices will do. For the manager, it's all Russian roulette. For the chief executive, with more than one thing in his life, it really isn't. So I would argue that someone with wide experience and distance from the scene should set prices in certain cases."[95]

Buffett joked about See's pricing power: "If you own See's Candies, and look in the mirror and say, 'Mirror, mirror on the wall, how much do I charge for candy this fall?' and it says, 'More', it's a good business."[96]

Pricing power illustrated

A very simple way to observe that Buffett and Munger's prior belief in the power of See's to raise prices was correct is to look at the amount of candy sold in 1972 and ten years later in 1982, while also looking at the sales and profit numbers.

Table 20.1 shows the price of a pound of candy went up 176% during a time of 137% of general inflation. Sales revenue quadrupled, mostly due to the increased price of candy, but also because of a 21% rise in the number of stores and an 18% creep-up in the number of pounds of candy sold in the typical store.

Table 20.1: See's pricing, revenue and profit, 1972 and 1982

	1972	1982	Increase (%)
Number of pounds of candy sold (millions)	17.0	24.2	42
Sales revenue	$31.3m	$123.7m	295
Profit after taxes	$2.3m	$12.7m	452
Number of stores	167	202	21
Sales revenue per pound of candy sold	$1.85	$5.11	176
Inflation over 11 years			137
Number of pounds of candy per store	101.8k	119.8k	18
Sales revenue per store	$187k	$612k	227

Source: Charles T. Munger and Donald A. Koeppel, Annual Report of Blue Chip Stamps (1982), p.34. Inflation data: inflationdata.com.

Sales revenue per store roughly trebled, but profit rose over five-fold. This was in part due to the increased selling prices but also because of the incredible downward pressure on operating costs. Apart from excellent management at every stage of the production, distribution and selling process, See's benefited from local economies of scale, particularly in:

- **Advertising** – for example, one newspaper or TV advertisement reached a large proportion of their customers in, say, San Francisco where there was clustering of shops, or around Los Angeles, their other big cluster.

- **Distribution** – candy was distributed from two factories in Los Angeles and San Francisco and predominantly delivered within 100 miles or so of the factories.

Munger (chairman) and Koeppel (president) wrote a glowing tribute in the 1982 Annual Report for Blue Chip Stamps:

"See's is by far the finest business we have ever purchased, exceeding our expectations, which were quite conservative. Our record as foretellers of the future is often poor, even with respect to businesses we have owned for many years, and we so greatly underestimated See's future that we were lucky to acquire it at all.

We believe that See's exceptional profits occur, mainly because both new and old customers prefer the taste and texture of See's candy, as well as the extremely high level of retailing service which characterizes its distribution. This customer enthusiasm is caused by See's virtually fanatic insistence on expensive natural candy ingredients plus expensive manufacturing and distributing methods that ensure rigorous quality control and cheerful retail service. These qualities are rewarded by extraordinary sales per square foot in the stores, frequently two to three times those of competitors, and by a strong preference by gift recipients for See's chocolates, even when measured against much more expensive brands."

In the early 1990s, See's had 218 stores, but instead of increasing the number of outlets they did the opposite and closed a dozen – each store must earn a satisfactory rate of return on capital employed. After 20 years of ownership, See's operated very efficiently with only $25m of net tangible assets in 1991. The initial assets of $8m were supplemented with only $18m of reinvested earnings. However, profits had risen ten-fold from 1971 to 1991, to reach $42.4m before tax, thus more than $20m after tax. Over those 20 years, See's distributed an amazing $410m to shareholders.

These numbers give insight into the quality of management at See's: to grow profits ten-fold the amount of capital tied up increased slightly over three-fold. The remainder of the profits were available for Blue Chip/Berkshire Hathaway to invest in other businesses with better prospects of a satisfactory percentage return than if the cash were used to open more See's shops in places where candy eaters would not pay a premium price. Buffett emphasised the strict objectivity needed to allocate this capital effectively in his 2014 letter to shareholders. He said:

> "We would have loved, of course, to intelligently use those funds to expand our candy operation. But our many attempts to do so were largely futile. So, without incurring tax inefficiencies or frictional costs, we have used the excess funds generated by See's to help purchase other businesses."[97]

By 1999 See's Candies was achieving an operating profit margin of 24%. For a food producer that is enormous. From 1972 to the end of 1999, it earned a total $857 million pre-tax. Buffett referred to the growth of the business in his usual jokey and yet wise manner:

> "Chuck gets better every year. When he took charge of See's at age 46, the company's pre-tax profit, expressed

in millions, was about 10% of his age. Today he's 74, and the ratio has increased to 100%. Having discovered this mathematical relationship – let's call it Huggins' Law – Charlie and I now become giddy at the mere thought of Chuck's birthday."[98]

Well, Huggins went on to achieve even greater things. To the end of 2014, See's total pre-tax earnings amounted to $1.9bn. Thus a purchase of $25m had given Buffett and Munger nearly $1bn after tax to invest in other businesses. In turn, these other businesses produced large distributable profits of their own. Buffett referred to it as being like "rabbits breeding".[99]

Buffett's ideas on what makes a good business

Here is a quiz for you: which is the better business?

Company A produced post-tax profits of $2m last year. Company B did the same.

Company A has only $8m of net tangible assets whereas Company B has five times as much, $40m of net tangible assets.

Profit growth is anticipated to be the same for both companies – in 20 years from now each will be producing $20m of profit after tax (a ten-fold increase on the profit today). They will also report the same profits in the years in between.

Make your choice now, before reading on.

Here is Buffett's logic

Company A is a candy manufacturer and retailer, whereas Company B is a steel manufacturer – it is a profitable steel producer with a good niche and so it can keep up with Company A in terms of profits reported in the annual report.

Note that to increase output and after-tax profits ten-fold, Company A would need to add to the initial net tangible assets

9 x $8m = $72m (assumption for the purposes of illustration). Thus after 20 years it is using $80m of capital.

To achieve a ten-fold increase in the output and profits of Company B, it would need to add 9 x $40m = $360m in net tangible assets. Say, nine more steel mills. Thus after 20 years it is using $400m of capital.

Company A over that 20 years can distribute to shareholders $288m ($360m - $72m) more than Company B to achieve the same annual profit in the final year.

So, despite the lower balance sheet value for Company A, it is more valuable. This is because it can do more of what investors want: passing on to them cash generated by the business. The steel mill company, on the other hand, has to use a high proportion of the money it generates in accounting profit to sustain the franchise and grow. With Company B, *owner earnings* (those earnings that can be paid out to shareholders without reducing volume of output, damaging the business franchise or forgoing value-generating investment projects within the firm) are less than *reported accounting earnings* (those drawn up by accountants each year for publication in the annual report) because of the need to invest so much cash.

How See's Candies illustrates economic goodwill

When it comes to reflecting the underlying reality of a business's position, accounting numbers often provide more confusion that enlightenment. It is important that we focus on the economic reality rather than statistics emanating from accounting rules.

Accounting rules usually dictate that a purchased business is examined to calculate the fair value of its assets after deduction of all its liabilities. In most cases this sum is much less than what was paid to acquire the business. That gives the accountant a problem: cash (or shares) was paid out of the holding company's balance sheet, but the fair value of net assets received in return is less. It would seem that value has just disappeared.

Of course, it has not disappeared; there might be very good reasons for paying a price much higher than the balance sheet fair value, say because the company has an excellent brand, lucrative patents or great relationships with customers. Thus we say that the extra amount paid above fair value is payment for *goodwill.*

But the accountant needs to deal with the technical form of goodwill – the difference between amount paid and fair value. This is put into the balance sheet as an asset. Usually accounting rules insist that accounting goodwill is regarded as declining year on year and so there is a gradual writing off. In the case of See's Candies, the rule at the time was for goodwill to be amortised over 40 years in equal annual amounts. This will reduce profit figures each year for 40 years, as well as balance sheet asset figures.

But this does not reflect economic reality. BCS paid $25m for See's, which had only $8m of net tangible assets. It was earning about $2m. See's Candies, like many businesses, earned rates of return on net tangible assets (at fair value) much higher than market rates of return – in the case of See's Candies the return on net tangible assets was 25% after tax ($2m return on $8m assets).

How was See's able to do this?

Answering this question brings us to the other type of goodwill: *economic goodwill.* The combination of balance sheet assets (inventory, machinery, etc.) and intangible assets (such as high reputation with consumers), produces the economic goodwill because it allows premium prices to be charged. Thus reputation can create a consumer franchise and a consumer franchise can create economic goodwill.

From the accountant's perspective, Blue Chip paid $17 million over net tangible assets. This amount had to be written off at $425,000 in each year over 40 years. Reported profits in the accounts were thus reduced by this amount.

From the perspective of someone valuing the business (such as an investor), we need to know if the economic franchise is declining. In the case of See's, profits grew and grew. In 1983, for example, $13m after tax was made. Amazingly, that was achieved with only $20m of net tangible assets. Thus we can say that See's economic goodwill was not *diminishing*, even as the accountant wrote down their type of goodwill (to about $12.5m in 1983). Customers still loved to buy See's candy and economic goodwill was still growing, so you can clearly see how the figures in the accounts become divorced from the reality of the business.

Both managers and investors have some rules to follow when considering goodwill, from the accounting perspective and from the economic value perspective:

- When looking at profits from a business unit ignore goodwill write offs and amortisation charges (annual deductions to allow for declining value of intangible fixed assets such as patents or depletion of a natural resource), so that the focus is on the return earned on the unleveraged (no borrowings) net tangible assets. This will guide judgement on the economic attractiveness of the operation and the current value of the operation's economic goodwill without the distortion of the accounting deductions for goodwill, etc.

- When trying to make a decision on the acquisition of a business ignore amortisation charges. They should not be deducted from earnings. This means that goodwill is viewed as continuing at its full cost.

- The cost of a business acquisition should be viewed as the entire intrinsic business value of all the payments made, whether they be in the form of cash or shares in the acquirer, not just the recorded accounting value. Value will not accrue to the acquirer if, despite being a very good company, an excessive price is paid for that economic goodwill.

Learning points

1. **Be in a position to buy inputs in a competitive market with many suppliers, but sell where you have pricing power.** Buffett said that if you can buy in a market that has been commoditised, (one with lots of sellers hawking a similar product), and sell to buyers that like the brand and are willing to pay a premium for it, then that "has long been a formula for business success… we have enjoyed good fortune with this approach at See's Candies since we purchased it 40 years ago."[100]

2. **Always praise your key managers.** Buffett regularly drew attention to Chuck Huggins's performance "and his fanatical insistence on both product quality and friendly service has rewarded customers, employees and owners."[101]

3. **Evaluate what is in the minds of customers.** See's was locked into the psyche of West Coasters. It "had a huge asset that did not appear on its balance sheet: a broad and durable competitive advantage that gave it significant pricing power."[102]

4. **Look for high returns on small amounts of capital.** The low levels of capital investment required to produce large increases in earnings at See's was a phenomenal combination.

5. **Pay-up for franchises.** At first Buffett and Munger were reluctant to pay a price so far above the net tangible asset value for See's. With hindsight, the high rates of return on capital meant that See's was cheap at $25m.

6. **Keep learning**. Buffett's experience of See's extraordinary growth reinforced his growing admiration of powerful brands. This led on to many other profitable investments.

Investment 21

WASHINGTON POST

Summary of the deal

Deal	Washington Post
Time	1974–present
Price paid	$10.6m (initially)
Quantity	9.7% of the company's shares
Sale price	Exchanged for a collection of businesses
Profit	Hundreds of millions of dollars

From the late 1960s, Buffett was frustrated in his search for shares at reasonable prices; he likened himself to a sex-starved man on a desert island.

He did manage to buy a few companies between 1970 and 1973 for Berkshire Hathaway, but the immediate results were not encouraging as he witnessed the portfolio market value falling: "We had significant unrealized depreciation – over $12 million – in our common stock holdings at year-end."[103]

This might have been a discouragement to Buffett at the time, but it will forever be an encouragement to those of us who experience long periods when Mr Market does not re-value what we think of as underpriced. Regardless, we should stick to our principles; value will out in the end.

Here is what Buffett told his BH shareholders in early 1974, following the portfolio mark-down to significantly below what he paid: "Nevertheless, we believe that our common stock portfolio at cost represents good value in terms of intrinsic business worth. In spite of the large unrealized loss at year-end, we would expect satisfactory results from the portfolio over the longer term."[104] Clearly he was not taking Mr Market's price as his benchmark for value.

He must have felt things were going a little slow. Newspapers didn't even bother to quote Berkshire's share price, despite it changing hands at over $80 by mid-1973, up from $40 in 1970. Even without the share portfolio yet to shoot the lights out, Buffett was content because he was able to report some good business results. In both 1972 and 1973, operating profits were over $11m. The insurance and reinsurance businesses were having "exceptionally fine" years on underwriting, providing not just zero-cost float but underwriting profits in abundance. The Illinois National Bank was adding record year to record year. Even textiles were producing profits "commensurate with our capital investment".[105]

On top of which, the overall investment portfolio, mostly in bonds, produced $6.8m in income in 1972 alone. BH's book value per share rose from $19.46 per share at the end of 1964 to over $70 in 1973.

Despite the business success, hardly anyone turned up to the annual general meeting of the company. Two that did make the journey were brothers Conrad and Edwin Taff. Conrad had been in Graham's class with Buffett. At least these three could keep the conversation going; they would spend hours discussing investment matters, starting a tradition of day-long questions and answers that continues to this day – the main difference being that 40,000 people now attend the AGM.

Nifty-Fifty

Buffett was finding it difficult to invest because a fashion had swept the market in the early 1970s, pushing shares to extraordinary levels. The sensible thing to do, apparently, was to buy shares in a group of 50 popular large capitalisation companies. Then you would have a bunch of solid buy-and-hold growth investments and could sleep soundly. They were said to be one-decision stocks because of their stability and demonstrated fast earnings growth. In fact, you should never sell.

But, many were selling on price-to-earnings ratios of 50 or above (they averaged 42) – how did it make sense to buy on 2% earnings yields? The word *growth* was the key. These companies were destined to grow their earnings per share at a fantastic rate and so the high share prices were entirely justified. There was no way they could let you down. This sentiment percolated through the market, until the vast majority of listed shares seemed pricey to Buffett.

Nifty-Fifty stocks included Avon, Polaroid and Xerox. True, these were good businesses, but were they good investments? The price-to-earnings ratios of these particular companies in late 1972 were 61, 95 and 46 respectively. Then, in early 1973, there was a small crack in confidence, with the Dow falling from around 1,000 to 900. Some shares fell much more, by 50% or so.

Then, in 1974, the real downturn came: the stock market collapsed nearly 50% in just two years. At the 1974 low point for Avon, its shares were down by 86%. Polaroid fell by 91% from its high and Xerox fell by 71%. Figure 21.1 illustrates this period for the Dow.

Figure 21.1: Dow Jones Industrial Average index (1968–75)

Buffett was not idle in periods of irrational exuberance

In early 1973, Buffett hired Salomon Brothers to raise $20m in senior notes (a bond) for BH, even though he did not need the cash for the operating business. This was partly to pay off an older debt of $9m, with the rest providing some extra firepower for the share portfolio when the time was right. The money came from 20 institutional investors and was due for redemption in 1993.

He had also busied himself analysing companies, despite not being able to take many buy decisions in the late 1960s and early 1970s. As shares fell in 1973 and 1974, portions of excellent business could be bought at bargain prices. Buffett was ready; he had done the preparation in the lean years and knew the quality of what he was now buying. He could pick up many shares at single-digit price-to-earnings ratios.

By mid-1974, deep pessimism had spread through the share-buying community, with people scared by simultaneous recession and 12% inflation (*stagflation*). But Buffett was in a totally different mood; he was having a great time. He was excited because he could pick up what others were throwing away. As he has said repeatedly: "Be fearful when others are greedy and be greedy when others are fearful."

In an interview conducted by Anthony Simpson, entitled 'Look At All Those Beautiful, Scantily Clad Girls Out There!', Buffett was asked "How do you contemplate the current stock market?"[106]

"Like an oversexed guy in a harem," he shot back. "This is the time to start investing."

The situation in 1974 reminded Buffett of the early 1950s when there was plenty of opportunity for the value investor. Among the American investing cognoscenti, Buffett was gaining respect as having a special level of knowledge. This was boosted by the fact that he had publically stated as long ago as the late 1960s, when everyone else was enthusiastic, that the market was doing irrational things. More than that, he had taken dramatic action by liquidating the partnership's portfolio. And, this prescience came after years of spectacularly outperforming the market.

You do not have to swing

As *Forbes* said, "Buffett is like the legendary guy who sold his stocks in 1928 and went fishing until 1933... He did 'go fishing' from 1969 to 1974. 'I call investing the greatest business in the world,' he says, 'because you never have to swing.' You stand at the plate, the pitcher throws you General Motors at 47! U.S. Steel at 39! And nobody calls a strike on you. There's no penalty except opportunity lost. All day you wait for the pitch you like; then when the fielders are asleep, you step up and hit it.' "[107]

Buffett tried to help other investors by setting out the key psychological stance needed to buy well. He advised that they should stay dispassionate and be patient – this applied when waiting for an overexcited market to calm down and also when buying into quality companies. At some point in the future the market price will reflect that high quality, so you hold on and wait.

Washington Post

The *Washington Post* newspaper routes, for which the 13-year-old Buffett rose early back in the 1940s, provided a large proportion of the $9,800 he saved in his teenage years. Who would have thought that this small amount of foundation capital would eventually lead to Buffett controlling the largest holding of *Washington Post* shares outside of the dominant family?

In spring and summer 1973, Buffett used some of the money he had raised for Berkshire Hathaway through the 20-year loan notes to buy shares in the Washington Post Company. The stake cost £10.6m and amounted to 9.7% of the overall equity capital of the firm. As well as the dominant *Post* newspaper, the company also owned *Newsweek*, four television stations, two radio stations, print mills and paper plants. All-told Buffett thought the business was worth $400m to $500m, while Mr Market priced it at $100m.

Before the deal

Katherine Graham was thrust into the role of leader of the Washington Post Company unexpectedly when aged 46 and she did not welcome it. Shy and diffident, with low self-confidence, her main preoccupation had previously been as a mother and homemaker. She knew nothing about management or editorial, but took it on as an obligation to maintain her legacy for the next generation of her family.

Her father had bought the *Washington Post* out of bankruptcy in 1933 and ran it as a privately-owned family firm. Later, Katherine's husband Philip Kay took over. It was only when Kay committed suicide in 1963 that Graham became president. The paper was then merely the third-placed Washington broadsheet.

The company did not float on the New York Stock Exchange (NYSE) until 1971. Even then, the family maintained voting control by holding onto its A shares, while raising money by issuing B shares that had much lower voting rights per share (the B shareholders were entitled to elect a maximum of 30% of the Board of Directors).

Brilliant journalism and fearless editorial leadership propelled the *Washington Post*. For example, the Nixon administration had deceived the American public regarding the origins of the Vietnam War. Unfortunately for them evidence of the government's decision-making was contained in what became known as the Pentagon Papers, which the *Post* published in the face of acute political anger and a law suit.

This was followed by another year of journalistic triumph, as its investigative reporters wrote articles about the Watergate scandal, defying veiled threats of violence from people with White House connections. Clearly the *Washington Post* was held in high regard, confirmed by Pulitzer prizes (47 at the last count), and grew to a paper of national and international standing.

While the paper had worldwide renown for integrity and excellence, business prospects were perceived to be fading in 1973. This feeling on Wall Street was created by the intense animosity emanating from the White House. There was talk of removing two TV licences in Florida, which between them accounted for about one-third of the company's earnings. Its shares fell.

Buffett's judgement on the value of the *Washington Post*

In 1985, Buffett stated: "Most security analysts, media brokers, and media executives would have estimated WPC's intrinsic business value at $400 to $500 million just as we did. And its $100 million stock market valuation was published daily for all to see."[108]

I would challenge Buffett a little on this statement, which came 12 years after the purchase – I wonder whether there was just a little bit of hindsight bias. The investment turned out well, so when Buffett looked back to 1973, it might have seemed obvious to all that it was worth a lot more than what he paid. But it may not have been so obvious at the time.

Imagine that you were valuing this company from the facts presented to you in the 1972 Annual Report, as shown in Table 21.1.

Table 21.1: Washington Post balance sheet (Dec 1972, $m)

Cash	10.2
Current financial assets	19.6
Receivables	25.2
Inventory	3.8
Prepayments	2.9
TOTAL OF CURRENT ASSETS	61.8
All liabilities	−81.9
NET CURRENT ASSET VALUE	−20.1

Source: Washington Post Company Annual Report (1972)

There is a negative net current asset value, so clearly this investment decision was not motivated by following Benjamin

Graham's net current asset value, NCAV, approach. What about the history of sales and profits? This is shown in Table 21.2.

Table 21.2: Washington Post revenue and net income (1965–72, $m)

	Revenue	Net income after tax
1965	108	7.7
1966	123	8.6
1967	131	7.1
1968	147	7.7
1969	169	8.5
1970	178	5.1
1971	193	7.2
1972	218	9.7

Source: Washington Post Company Annual Report 1972

Are you seeing a valuation near to the $400m–$500m that Buffett claimed in 1985? Nor me.

There was some growth in the profit numbers, but not that much, and besides which they were all less than $10m, so we would be talking of a price-to-earnings ratio of 40–50. This sort of ratio gives most value investors a nosebleed.

Let's try looking at the year 1972 in more detail, in Table 21.3.

Table 21.3: Washington Post income from operations before tax (1971–72, $m)

	1972	1971	Growth
Newspapers	10.2	8.7	17%
Magazines and books	5.7	2.7	107%
Broadcasting	5.9	3.8	58%

Looking at those growth numbers, I am getting a little closer. Something extraordinary might have been happening at this company. How did it raise income by so much? Did it acquire firms? (It did not.)

If not, how did it grow organically, and are those fundamentals of the business sustainable over decades? If so, I might have accepted a much higher price-to-earnings ratio than 10.

Before I look at the events of the year and the qualitative factors, another important set of data is shown in Table 21.4.

Table 21.4: Washington Post revenue by customer type (1971–72, $m)

	1972	1971
Advertising	166	148
Circulation (paid by readers or viewers)	47	42
Other	4	3

Over three-quarters of revenue came from advertising. Put yourself in the position of, say, a furniture store advertiser or a whisky brand-manager. Where do you want to advertise most:

in the paper with over 60% of the circulation in the town, or the paper with a fraction of that market share?

Of course, you'd be willing to pay a lot more to place your ad in the dominant paper. Thus, over the years, the dominant paper can reap greatly increased income without spending much more on editorial or management. The same logic applies to TV advertising and to the market leader in weekly paper news, which was *Newsweek*.

But just how strong are those franchises? Let's take each of the divisions in turn.

Washington Post

In July 1972, the newspaper market in Washington changed dramatically. *The Washington Daily News* ceased publication. That meant that this important city – according to the Washington Post Company's 1972 annual report, "the nation's fastest-growing, wealthiest, best-educated and most news-hungry" – was left with only two dailies, the *Washington Post* (WP) and the *Washington Star-News*.

Of those two, the WP was the most dominant, with 63% of all advertising and three out of every five adults reading it daily. When it came to the Sunday edition, two-thirds of the adult population read the *Post*. Daily circulation of the *Post* had risen by one-third over the past 15 years, with Sunday circulation rising by an enormous two-thirds.

Thus we have a dominant paper in the most influential city in the US with a growing appetite for quality journalism. As the annual report said, "Gains in advertising and circulation promise to continue." With that degree of entrenchment and growth prospects I would be willing to pay a much higher multiple of last year's earnings than the level of 10 that Mr Market offered at the time.

Ask the question: would you rather wrestle with grizzlies than try to compete with the *Washington Post* in its home market in 1973? If the answer is yes, you can see that this paper had a strong economic franchise. Where else could advertisers go?

Newsweek

In the field of weekly news, the jointly dominant publication was *Newsweek*, alongside *Time*. *Newsweek* was out in front in terms of advertising pages. Advertising revenue reached a new high in 1972, climbing to $72.5m. In the US market, 2,725,000 copies were sold in a typical week. Also, 375,000 were sold in 150 other countries. It had branched out into *Newsweek Books*, which by 1973 was "a sizable and profitable business".[109] Profits of the Newsweek division more than doubled in one year.

Again, ask the question: would you like to set up a rival to try to compete against that degree of reader recognition and respect built up over generations by *Newsweek*?

Broadcasting

Back in the 1970s, TV stations were licences to print money because of the local monopoly/oligopoly power granted. At the 1972 year end, the Washington Post Company had four of these, but was close to purchasing its fifth. It also had two radio stations. The 1972 annual report played down the significance of the franchises (perhaps to avoid alerting the authorities to potential returns on capital due to high advertising rates): "our three television and two radio stations achieved healthy competitive positions in their respective markets. As we move through the first quarter of 1973 I am extremely optimistic... we have reached a takeoff point which should result in new successes in both journalistic and programming output, as well as our financial results."

Even if you wanted to try to compete with these stations you could not, because you would not get a licence.

The shift in philosophy is complete

What this case study illustrates is that in 1973 Buffett placed a tremendous amount of value on the strength of the economic franchise and quality of management, leading to expectations of high future earnings growth. Here there was virtually no balance sheet contribution to the buy decision, except that financial gearing and liquidity risk were absent.

So while Buffett was somewhat influenced by the balance sheet in the case of See's Candies, in the case of the Washington Post Company he found the franchise prospects so mouth-watering that he only needed to know that the balance sheet was not dangerous. What he focused on was 95% qualitative: things like reader's high regard for *Newsweek* and the *Washington Post*, and their emotional attachment to their local TV and radio stations. On the back of that, the dividend had recently doubled and the directors were talking about healthy growth prospects.

Was Buffett foolishly optimistic?

When it comes down to it, it does not matter whether Buffett was right or wrong on the $400m–$500m valuation.

When he was buying at a market capitalisation of $100m he had a very large margin of safety, whether the true value turned out to be $200m or $500m. I think we would all agree that the business was worth at least $200m (assuming the White House didn't close down the *Post*), so at a market capitalisation of $100m it could be picked up at half price or less.

The quality of franchise and management made it a remarkably safe investment at $10.6m for 10% of the future earnings and dividends.

The deal

After accumulating slightly over 5% of *Washington Post's* shares in late spring 1973, Buffett wrote to Katherine Graham to say he would like to buy more. She was terrified that a raider would take the company out of family hands or influence it for political purposes and so she did not receive this letter from Omaha with much affection.

While the warmth that Buffett put in the letter, with its focus on praising quality journalism and his long admiration for the *Washington Post* since childhood, helped calm her down a little, she was still afraid. Graham was told by friends and advisors that, logically, there was no way she could lose control of the company no matter how many shares Berkshire Hathaway bought, because the publically traded B shares had so little voting power. The best that a buyer could hope for, even if they bought a majority of the Bs, was to get just one seat on the board. She still controlled all the A shares.

Buffett won Katherine Graham round

Graham agreed to meet Buffett. It wasn't long before his intelligence, decency and humour won her over. At a second meeting, in the autumn, Buffett made it plain that takeover was not an option. He charmed her and they became lifelong friends.

Berkshire Hathaway bought 467,150 shares of Washington Post B stock at a cost of $10.6m. The shares were shortly afterwards split to be 934,300 shares. In 1979 they were split again to become 1,868,000 shares, then reduced slightly by buy-backs. Overall, there were 4.8m shares in circulation (As and Bs) in 1973.

To reassure Graham, Buffett agreed, in writing, not to buy any more unless she gave permission. Note his willingness to buy into a company when he had little voting power. If he trusted the key people, he was no longer worried about control. Later Buffett arranged for Graham's son, Don, to vote as BH's proxy on his shares in WP – he thought Don very smart as well as trustworthy.

What happened after the purchase?

Promptly, the company that Buffett thought was worth $400m–$500m witnessed Mr Market in a foul mood. This low-debt, quality franchise company *fell* in market value from around $100m to only about $80m; one-fifth of its estimated intrinsic value. A crippling strike did not help, on top of the Watergate fallout with threats to its TV licences. During the strike Graham and Buffett worked side-by-side wrapping up newspapers into bundles and pasting labels by hand, often until 3am. They would go home filthy and exhausted.

Eventually things got straightened out; the strike was settled and Nixon's administration crumbled. But it was not until three years after purchase that Berkshire Hathaway's shares in the Washington Post Company climbed back to the level at which Buffett had bought.

Graham leaned heavily on her new friend from Omaha, who she quickly recognised offered much wisdom regarding business and investment. Buffett was more than willing to allow her to draw from his well of experience and rationality. He also boosted her confidence by telling her how smart she was, which he truly believed. So close was the relationship that she even asked Buffett to help her write speeches to groups such as Wall Street professionals. Buffett also gave Graham lessons in accounting.

Once again, we see Buffett clearly identifying the key person for one of his businesses and then nurturing that individual as a friend and leader. He did not second-guess Graham's operational decisions, but supported them with advice when requested, praised work well done and offered a listening ear when difficult decisions had to be made.

In this case, Buffett had no real power as a shareholder, but he did have influence because Graham trusted him as a confidant and shrewd businessman. As his influence grew, his status morphed into greater power after he was invited to join the board in autumn 1974, a position he thoroughly enjoyed. The memory of starting out as a newspaper delivery boy and now finding himself in a leadership role made it all the sweeter. He was fascinated by journalism, even going so far as to say if he had not followed an investment career he would most likely have been a journalist.

As one of her best friends, Buffett would stay in Graham's home once a month prior to board meetings, becoming a familiar presence to her four children, who took to him like an uncle.

Buffett stepped down from the board of WP in 1986 because he wanted a directorship at Capital Cities, a very successful media group Berkshire had bought into. The media regulator did not allow a person to be a director of two companies if one has television networks and the other has cable television systems. Buffett figured he could retain influence at the Washington Post Company without being on the board. When Capital Cities was sold to Disney in 1996, Buffett returned to the WP board.

Holding on to silk purses

In 1987, almost every share in the Berkshire portfolio was sold, except for three. One of the chosen three was Washington Post. In his 1987 letter to shareholders, Buffett explained his logic for holding on to these three companies even when the market was forcing share prices to expensive levels: "we view these investments exactly like our successful controlled businesses – a permanent part of Berkshire rather than merchandise to be disposed of once Mr. Market offers us a sufficiently high price." He said that this approach fitted the personalities of Charlie Munger and himself, and how they wanted to live their lives. He wanted to work with people he strongly liked and admired even if that meant missing some financial return.

The three companies were Capital Cities/ABC, Inc in which slightly over £0.5 billion had been invested (then worth $1bn in 1987), GEICO which had cost $45.7m but was worth $757m in 1987, and Washington Post, worth $323m in 1987.

The logic was the same whether buying a business that could be completely controlled or a minority stake in stock market traded company: "In each case we try to buy into businesses with favorable long-term economics. Our goal is to find an outstanding business at a sensible price, not a mediocre business at a bargain price. Charlie and I have found that making silk purses out of silk is the best that we can do; with sow's ears, we fail."[110]

The contribution of Washington Post to Berkshire Hathaway

An investment of $10.6m grew to have a market worth of over $1,300m by 2005, excluding the dividends received. But note how patient Buffett had to be with Mr Market: it wasn't until 1981 that the market valued the company at the $400m–$500m Buffett had placed on the business in 1973. Figure 21.2 shows the rewards the Post delivered to BH over the period from 1973 to 2008.

As we all know, in the last decade newspapers have been having a hard time of it and so the share price of WP slid in this period. Even allowing for the recent downturn, this investment has returned many times the amount Buffett put in. For example, by the turn of the millennium the annual dividend had reached the same figure as the amount Berkshire had paid for each share. And still today Berkshire Hathaway benefits from TV station income. Figure 21.3 shows the Washington Post Company (now Graham Holdings Company, GHC) share price for 1990 to 2016. Berkshire Hathaway paid about $5 per share (allowing for share splits).

Figure 21.2: Rewards to BH from Washington Post Company

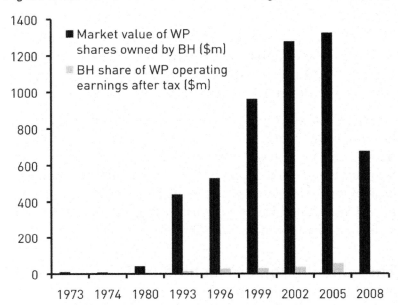

Source: Berkshire Hathaway Chairman's Letters; Washington Post Company Annual Reports

Buffett's managerial themes at the Washington Post Company

As a director of the Washington Post Company, Buffett was able to share his insights on good managerial practice. Here we consider some of his contributions to shaping the company.

Share buy-backs

One thing Buffett pressed for was share repurchases. He persuaded the board that when the price was low enough, it made great sense for a company to buy its own shares from the market. That way, earnings per share could rise, lifting the value of each remaining

Figure 21.3: Graham Company Holdings share price (1990–2016)

Source: Yahoo Finance

share: the discounted future annual owner earnings were split between fewer shares, increasing the present value.

This can be done when shares are selling below intrinsic value, conservatively calculated. The company must have the funds available either in cash or through sensible borrowing, which would not otherwise be needed for investment within the business in value-creating projects.

Over the years, about half of Washington Post's shares were repurchased. As a result, Berkshire Hathaway ownership rose from 10% in 1973 to over 18% by 1999, without it buying any further shares.

Takeovers and start-ups

Buffett also restrained the board from paying high prices in bidding wars for hot media assets – it was simply not necessary to keep up with the Joneses when excitement for newspaper titles, TV or cable franchises was feverish. It was better to keep hold of the cash.

This parsimony, and Buffett's hold over Katherine Graham, frustrated many of the more expansionist senior managers and directors. But new ideas and start-up ventures were not what the Washington Post Company was all about in Buffett's eyes. He saw it as a low-risk producer of a flow of owner earnings from its base of solid and enduring business franchises, and not a vehicle for speculating on a new-fangled idea that might just work… or might not.

Even if the media and tech guys thought something was very promising, for example a 24-hour news channel, Buffett was cautious if he felt it was outside his circle of competence, and even more cautious if he thought it was outside the management's circle of competence.

Opportunities were undoubtedly missed, but nevertheless the returns on capital within the Washington Post Company's various businesses were high, and this meant that the returns on the shares were excellent. These returns could be obtained without the fear of backing the wrong horse and losing it all in the game of speculation about the future.

Buffett is very keen on companies sticking to those business areas where they have a distinct competitive advantage, giving pricing power and high returns on capital. Any surplus capital generated by a company should only be retained to invest in new schemes if there is reasonable certainty that it can generate a satisfactory rate of return for each dollar put in; the rest should flow to shareholders to place elsewhere. Growth in size as measured by turnover, market capitalisation or profits is not the goal; high return on capital is.

This mindset meant that over the next few decades the Washington Post Company strayed very little from the form and structure that Buffett found when he started buying its shares. It tried out a few ideas, such as a sports magazine, but this was small beer relative to the original franchises of *Washington Post, Newsweek* and the collection of television stations, which continued to account for the bulk of the profits.

An Inevitable

Buffett described the *Washington Post* as an "Inevitable". These are the best type of firms to own (but only if you can buy at the right price), because they dominate their industries or segments of their industries. More importantly, they can reasonably be expected to dominate in decades from now because of their extraordinary competitive strengths.

One way of getting straight in your mind whether a company you are examining is an Inevitable is to imagine going to live on a desert island for ten years; will that firm still dominate its industry when you get back? Kellogg's will probably be a dominant player in cereals ten years from now; Coca-Cola in drinks; Gillette in razors; Cadbury in chocolate. Their power comes from what is in the mind of the consumer and that affection can last generations.

But will Apple be dominant in smartphones, BMW in cars and Walmart in retailing? Arguably, these have fairly high probabilities of still being strong, but not high enough to be regarded as Inevitables because there is too much potential for consumers to turn to alternatives. The smartphone market is vulnerable to yet more disruption, the premium car market has many players for buyers to choose from and BMW has to remain at the top of its game every year, and Walmart is under attack from Amazon, let alone other traditional retailers.

Donald Graham: the second key person

Katherine's son, Donald, a Harvard graduate, Vietnam veteran and former policeman did not join the family firm until he was 26 in 1971, as a lowly reporter. He worked his way up, becoming executive vice president, then publisher of the newspaper. All the while, his mother retained her positions of chairman of the board and CEO. It was not until 1991 that Donald was made CEO of the holding company; the chairmanship followed in 1993. Despite his modest persona and gentle managerial style, Don Graham has an excellent business brain and a phenomenal memory.

He greatly admires his friend Buffett and is strongly influenced by his ideas. Buffett is always there for counsel when Don is dealing with key business decisions. The themes of his leadership approach are familiar to us:

- Focus on long-term returns to shareholders rather than short-term concerns.

- Constantly bear down on costs and cut out the frills (e.g. no company cars and cheap industrial carpets).

- Find managers you trust and delegate.

- Grow your own senior people by nurturing them over a long period and promoting them.

- When buying businesses, pay for quality but never overpay, and expect to hold for the very long term.

- Get the company to buy back its own shares when it has surplus cash and the shares are cheap.

The loss of franchise value

Even Inevitables can stop being dominant eventually. The *Washington Post* is a case in point. The alternative advertising media of the internet and 24-hour news channels has played havoc with the strength of its franchise.

For decades things were fine. After Berkshire Hathaway had held its shares for 14 years the Washington Post Company reported an amazing net income (after tax) of $269m in 1988. Remember, this is a company that had a market capitalisation of only $80m 14 years before. In 1998 net income peaked at $417m.

But like thousands of newspapers around the world, even this excellent franchise was destroyed by disruptive new technology. The newspaper and magazine publishing parts of the Washington Post Company became unprofitable. At first the decline was slow, but in the 21st century newspaper revenue slid and losses were made, despite efforts at cost containment.

In 2010, *Newsweek* was sold for $1, with the buyer, Sidney Harman, taking on its pension and other liabilities. In 2013 Jeff Bezos, founder of Amazon, bought the *Washington Post* newspaper. The Graham family had come to the conclusion that, while the paper would survive under their control, it would do much better with Bezos adding his technical and marketing touch. Bezos paid $250m for it and vowed to maintain its tradition of independent journalism.

What was left?

The vast majority of the value of the company remained following the sales of *Newsweek* and the *Post* newspaper. For a long time, the paper and *Newsweek* had been insignificant earners and generators of shareholder value. Under the continued leadership of Don Graham, the Washington Post Company owned cable-TV systems, TV stations, online businesses, print works and local TV news outfits. The most significant business, however, was the education and training company, Kaplan. This had been bought in 1984 for $40m, but by 2007 Kaplan was responsible for about 50% of the revenue of a company now valued by the stock market at $3bn. It was considered sensible to change the name of the company following the sale of the paper, so it became known as Graham Holdings.

Buffett made a move

In March 2014, Berkshire Hathaway agreed a deal with Graham Holdings by which Berkshire ended up owning WPLG, a Miami-based television station (Buffett had left the board of WPC in 2011). In the deal, Berkshire also received shares in itself (BH) that Graham Holdings had bought years before, and cash.

This was all in exchange for approximately 1.6m shares of Graham Holdings Class B shares owned by Berkshire Hathaway. By this time, the 1.6m shares accounted for about 28% of the shares outstanding, thus Graham Holdings was effectively conducting a share buy-back, but instead of paying all cash it also handed BH one of its valuable franchises. Berkshire, too, effectively did a share buy-back by receiving shares in itself from Graham Holdings. Following the deal, Berkshire still held about 127,000 shares in Graham Holdings.

The whole deal gave a value of about $1.1bn on the shares Buffett sold back to Graham Holdings. Berkshire had already received many times the $10.6m it paid for the Washington Post Company four decades earlier. Now it held the dominant TV station covering the 16th largest market in the US, with 1.66m TV homes. WPLG is an affiliate of Walt Disney Co.'s ABC.

Buffett's reflections on one of his greatest investments – and a dig at academics and their acolytes

In Buffett's 1985 letter to Berkshire Hathaway shareholders, he observed how foolish Mr Market can be, the importance of strong media industry franchises and his willingness to hold much-loved companies even if future returns were destined to be less than they gave in the past.

He repeated his observation that in mid-1973, the Washington Post Company was worth $400–$500 but was selling for $100m.

"Our advantage... was attitude: we had learned from Ben Graham that the key to successful investing was the purchase of shares in good businesses when market prices were at a large discount from underlying business values."[111]

Other analysts were not focused on analysing the business; they were "under the spell of academics at prestigious business schools who were preaching a newly-fashioned theory: the stock market was totally efficient, and therefore calculations of business value – and even thought, itself – were of no importance in investment activities."[112][113]

Buffett gave praise to Katherine Graham for having the intelligence and courage to both build the business and to buy back large quantities of shares at the bargain prices offered in 1974 – at 25% below what Berkshire had paid.

Gradually, very gradually, other investors realised that this business had exceptional economics and the share price increased: "Thus, we experienced a triple dip: the company's business value soared upward, per-share business value increased considerably faster because of stock repurchases and, with a narrowing of the discount, the stock price outpaced the gain in per-share business value."

The churn rate of a portfolio

As we have seen. Buffett held his investment in the Washington Post Company for many years. In his 1986 letter to Berkshire shareholders, Buffett pointed out the virtues of an extended holding period of a number of years, or even decades. He argued that such an attitude provides:

- A buttress against following the Wall Street fad of the moment pushing you to dump shares.

- Strength of mind when confronted with temporary operating problems, preventing irrational fear, and maintenance of gaze on the long term.

- Immunisation against becoming too enamoured by a new corporate concept, such as computers and software in 1986 or dotcoms or social media today.

- Time to be a true investor, that is time to analyse the underlying business. Frantic traders cannot do this.

- A stable and trusting environment for operating managers to plan their businesses for value creation in the long run, knowing that an interested and supportive major shareholder will not cut and run. The psychological impact of this should not be underestimated; it engenders loyalty, focus on the long term, knowledgeable two-way interaction and honesty.

In the letter, Buffett wrote:

> "We should note that we expect to keep permanently our three primary holdings, Capital Cities/ABC, Inc., GEICO Corporation, and The Washington Post. Even if these securities were to appear significantly overpriced, we would not anticipate selling them, just as we would not sell See's or Buffalo Evening News if someone were to offer us a price far above what we believe those businesses are worth.

> ...we will stick with our 'til-death-do-us-part policy. It's the only one with which Charlie and I are comfortable, it produces decent results, and it lets our managers and those of our investees run their businesses free of distractions."[114]

Learning points

I. **Look through temporary problems to the quality of the franchise when estimating intrinsic value.**

2. **Do not be disheartened if the share falls after purchase.**
Intrinsic value is likely to remain the same – and it might
even have risen!

3. **Keep holding if high returns on capital employed are
likely.** Do not sell too soon just because you have bagged a
paper profit.

4. **Share buy-backs are good for shareholders if the price is
low enough.** Earnings per share can rise, lifting the value of
each remaining share.

5. **Do not pay high prices in bidding wars for hot businesses.**
If everyone else is excited, you do not have to be.

6. **Inevitables are the best type of firms to own** (when bought
at the right price) because they dominate their industries
or segments of their industries, and are likely to dominate
years from now because of their extraordinary competitive
strengths.

7. **High-quality economic franchises can disappear** (e.g.
newspapers), so be prepared to reallocate capital to new areas
with ongoing strong franchises (e.g. TV stations or education
in the case of the Washington Post).

8. **Do not churn your portfolio.** High rates of change in
portfolio constituents will please your broker and the taxman,
but damage your wealth.

Investment 22

WESCO FINANCIAL

Summary of the deal

Deal	Wesco Financial
Time	1974–present
Price paid	Around $17 per share
Quantity	Initially 64% of the company's shares for about $30m
Sale price	Still held
Profit	Over $2bn

The Wesco Financial story is most interesting not for the subsequent success of the original business, but for the clever things that Buffett and Munger did with the resources held within the firm over the 30 years from when they bought the business. Instead of leaving the bulk of the money to support a savings and loan organisation providing mortgages, they followed the path trodden by Berkshire Hathaway by buying and building up other important businesses, such as in insurance, and they invested in a portfolio of stock market shares, bonds and preferred stock, ranging from RJ Reynolds to Wells Fargo.

Indeed, many Buffett followers referred to Wesco as a mini-Berkshire due to its mix of wholly-owned operating businesses, especially insurance, and its collection of tradable securities, many of which were common to both Berkshire's and Wesco's portfolios. A major attraction for small investors wanting to ride on Buffett and Munger's coat-tails was that Wesco's shares could be picked up for tens of hundreds of dollars each, whereas Berkshire's rose into the tens of thousands. It was a cheaper way in.

There was the added bonus that Wesco shareholders were invited to its annual general meeting, presided over by Charlie Munger. Attendees were guaranteed to walk away from the meetings held in Wesco's cafeteria in Pasadena, California, with inspirational pearls of wisdom.

The business

Wesco Financial was the holding company for the Mutual Savings and Loans Association of Pasadena. This was founded in the 1920s by Rudolph W. Caspers. It did well in the building boom following the second world war and floated its shares on the American Stock Exchange in 1959.

But from then until 1972, while it was regarded as well managed, with high vigilance over costs and decent profits, it was viewed as sleepy and not bound for fast growth. Its shares drifted into the low teens.

By then the key shareholders were various descendants of Rudolph W. Casper, but even between them they did not own a majority. This group was led by Elizabeth 'Betty' Caspers Peters. She served on the board but otherwise this 47-year-old attended to her school-aged children and farmland in the fertile Napa Valley. Today, she is still on the board, now a 90-year-old. Another key person in this story, Louis R. Vincenti, joined Wesco in 1955. He quickly worked his way up to become president by 1961.

Munger and Buffett became interested

For some time, Buffett had taken a keen interest in savings and loan companies. He had read hundreds of their reports and accounts. In the summer of 1972, Wesco Financial had a market capitalisation under $30m, which was about one-half of the net asset value. Buffett and Munger instructed Blue Chip Stamps to buy 8% of the shares for about $2m.

In the second half of 1972, Betty Caspers Peters encouraged the board to be more dynamic and grow the business. The other directors rejected her advice and gave the impression of condescension. In frustration, she became open to the idea of merging the organisation with another that had more executive *get-up-and-go*. Financial Corporation of Santa Barbara seemed to fit the bill as they were busy opening branches and generally doing what Betty thought should be done at Wesco, that is taking steps to grow larger.

A bad offer was made

In January 1973, Wesco announced that it planned to merge with Santa Barbara Savings and Loan. Elizabeth Caspers Peters was aware that the offer was not all that great, but felt that something had to be done.

The 8% shareholders over at Blue Chip's California headquarters and in Omaha were incensed that Wesco executives were giving so much away, by offering too many Wesco shares for Santa Barbara shares. A plan was hatched to stop the merger.

Warren Buffett's takeover of Wesco Financial

Buffett and Munger came up with a two-pronged strategy. First, Blue Chip needed to increase its voting rights. It bought more shares, paying up to $17, until it had 17% (regulators prevented an unapproved shareholding of more than 20% in S&L companies).

Second, they needed to persuade members of the board that this merger was not in the best interests of shareholders. Munger asked for a meeting with Wesco's CEO, Louis Vincenti, but was politely told that the deal would go ahead if shareholders approved following a recommendation from the board. The rebuffed Munger then looked to Betty Caspers Peters. At first Don Koeppel, President of Blue Chip, spoke to Peters, but he was sent away. Then Buffett phoned. Fortunately, she had just finished reading about Buffett and his Graham-based philosophy in the book *Supermoney*,[115] in which he was described as a clear thinker, full of business wisdom. Suitably impressed, Peters agreed to meet Buffett only 24 hours later.

They met in a lounge at San Francisco airport. While they hit it off straightaway, Peters made it plain that she wanted something done at Wesco. Buffett asked if, instead of the merger, he might be allowed to give it a try. He was convinced that he could generate more value for shareholders.

But what if Buffett was incapacitated, or run over by a bus and killed? Where would her and her brother's shares be then? Well, Buffett said, Charlie Munger would be a fine person to take over. After all, Buffett trusted Munger's intelligence and integrity to such a degree that he had already arranged for him to manage Berkshire Hathaway and his family shareholdings if Buffett became no longer able to. After three hours it was agreed that Peters would lobby the board for a cessation of merger plans.

Following a second meeting, this time with Munger as well as Buffett, Peters was willing to press the board to arrange a meeting with the two of them. When she attempted this she found a determination to go ahead with the merger rather than discuss it further. Annoyed, she asked her family to vote against it.

Buffett and Munger launched into action

The merger plan was defeated by a shareholder vote and the directors were angry. The share price fell from around $17 to $11.

Buffett and Munger sped into action. They first jumped over various regulatory hurdles to free them to buy more than 20% of the shares in Wesco. Then they made several tender offers to other shareholders and raised Blue Chip's stake to one-quarter of the shares.

They offered more than the market price, at $17. Especially in light of a general stock market decline, this was an extraordinary thing to do. They were generous on the price so that it would not seem that they caused the merger to fail simply so that they could pick up shares at falling prices in the aftermath.

Apart from common decency and the honour code by which these two operated, Buffett and Munger needed to gain the respect, trust and dedication of Louis Vincenti, who they had already identified as their key person at Wesco.

They had scuttled the very merger that he had recommended; the least they could do was offer other shareholders an exit at the pre-collapse price. That way Vincenti could see that the shareholders he had served for many years, many of whom were friends, were treated fairly. Buffett and Munger saw Vincenti as straight-talking, shrewd, independent and honourable, though cranky, and they wanted him to be their long-term *partner*. There is that concept again – partnership – incorporating traits such as trust, respect, integrity and mutual enrichment.

Over the first half of 1974, Blue Chip bought enough shares to declare it had a majority. Betty Caspers Peters continued as a minority shareholder, a decision that she later regarded as one of the most fortunate she ever made as Wesco was transformed.

The early struggle with Wesco

Buffett and Munger joined the Wesco board in 1974, while Blue Chip continued to purchase shares – by the end of 1974 it had 64% of Wesco. It wasn't until 1977 that it held 80%, the limit agreed with Betty Caspers Peters.

Wesco performed well. For example, the 80% of its profits after tax attributable to Blue Chip amounted to $5.715m in 1977, which is a pretty good return on the amount paid of somewhere between $30m and $40m.[116]

It's interesting to note that it was not just improved performance in the savings and loans business that boosted earnings, but capital gains were significant from a strong balance sheet that showed "substantial assets outside its subsidiary savings and loan association and available for commitment elsewhere."[117]

The following year, 1978, the 80% of Wesco's net income attributable to Blue Chip jumped up to $7,417,000. It happened to be a very good year for savings and loan associations, but this was not to last.

Note that Berkshire Hathaway did not benefit from Wesco's profits to the full extent of $7.417m because at that time BH held only 58% of Blue Chip which, in turn, owned 80% of Wesco Financial Corporation. Thus, Berkshire's equity in Wesco's earnings was about 46%. It was not until 1983 that Berkshire Hathaway owned 100% of Blue Chip Stamps.

A steely move

We've already seen that some of the funds held within the company were being used to invest in securities, but until February 1979 Wesco had only the one operating business. Then it was joined by a Midwestern steel service centre business called Precision Steel Warehouse Inc., located in the outskirts of Chicago, which was purchased for approximately $15m. As well as selling lengths of metal, Precision Steel manufactured and distributed tool room supplies and other products sold under its own brand names.

Precision Steel reported after-tax earnings of $1,918,000 for 1978, so the price of only $15m seemed pretty good. However, steel suppliers operate in highly competitive markets, subject more than most to the ups and downs of the economy. For the next few years profits fell. At first, the decline was slight, but in the last quarter of 1981 a severe recession in the steel industry began and profits plunged. In 1982, only $0.3m after tax was made.

The recession-induced decline was exacerbated by what Munger and Koeppel described in their 1982 Blue Chip letter as "a business mistake". They said they should never have entered the small measuring-tool distribution business. This Precision Steel subsidiary was closed down in 1982 "at substantial cost". Quite frankly, this was a less than auspicious beginning for a mini-conglomerate.

However, the storms were weathered, and Precision Steel is still owned by Wesco today. But it has suffered from many years of famine, with only a few years of feast. For example, in the late 1990s it had a row of years when after-tax profits reached giddy heights exceeding $3m. This was followed by a four-year period of approximately break-even. All in all, we have to look at the Precision Steel investment as one of the least profitable uses of money under the command of Buffett and Munger.

Savings and loan disaster

So, in the early 1980s Wesco had a struggling steel operation and the original savings and loan (S&L) business, plus a portfolio of securities. But the S&L started to present managerial challenges for Buffett and Munger. As early as spring 1980, the chiefs in charge of Blue Chip, and therefore Wesco, Charlie Munger and Donald Koeppel, were warning of the possibility of poor prospects for the entire S&L industry. A very serious problem had arisen because S&Ls generally offered borrowers fixed-rate mortgages stretching over decades. This money came from depositors offered floating rates. Furthermore, depositors were allowed to withdraw their money at short notice.

As inflation and general interest rates rose in the early 1980s, S&Ls were obliged to offer ever-increasing interest rates to attract deposits. But they were prevented from raising interest rates on the mortgages to offset this because of the fixed-rate deals they had signed up to. Thus they could end up charging less to borrowers than they paid depositors. Many became insolvent.

This is where the wider perspective on economic matters, and a deep knowledge of a range of business areas, held by Buffett, Munger and Koeppel, resulted in a clever positioning of Wesco – not only to survive the crisis, but to thrive. They recognised early that profits at Mutual Savings could plummet. So in March 1980, they sold to Brentwood Savings and Loan Association all of Mutual's offices except its headquarters building and "a satellite thereto to be opened across the street".

Prior to the sale, Mutual had over $480m of deposits. About $300m of these were transferred to Brentwood, together with offsetting mortgage loans in equal amounts. This smart move:

- reduced exposure to the S&L market by almost two-thirds at a time when a storm was about to break

- raised money by selling physical branch offices

- lowered the ongoing costs of serving customers holding the remaining $150m or so of mortgages and about $170m in deposits, because the branch network had gone

- kept safe a pot of money (about $104m) held in cash, securities and deposits earning interest for Wesco. That was yet another substantial fund for Buffett and Munger to allocate on top of those in Berkshire's insurance subsidiaries and Blue Chip Stamp's accounts.

In selling off the majority of the business, it was made clear that this was not a statement that there definitely would be a devastating rise in interest rates, but that it was wise to protect the downside should interest rates rise. Munger and Koeppel wrote the following to Blue Chip shareholders in March 1980:

"If, some time within the next few years, inflation and interest rates rise significantly and more or less permanently, the sale of branch offices will much improve aggregate future earnings. Thus Mutual Savings has taken action designed to protect itself from adverse effects of high inflation rather than action to position itself for maximum profit from low inflation. The action taken was not based on the belief that high inflation and high interest rates in the future are inevitable, or even more likely than not. Instead the action reflects a desire, motivated by the margin-of-safety considerations intrinsic in engineering and still appropriate, we think, in financial institutions, to restructure Mutual Savings so that a sort of 'earthquake risk' was reduced."

I regard their prescience in conceiving of a major S&L crisis, and their decisiveness in taking action to limit its impact on Mutual, as brilliant. They had set up the company for a very prosperous future.

The transformation started

Some of the money released was sent up the ownership chain. Indeed, by early 1982, almost as much as Blue Chip had paid for its 80% stake had been received from Wesco in the form of dividends. This is shown in Table 22.1. This was put to very good use, buying controlling interests and non-controlling interests in some great companies.

Table 22.1: Blue Chip's average equity and share of Mutual Savings cash dividend (1975–81)

Year	Blue Chip's average equity in Mutual Savings as carried in Blue Chip's consolidated balance sheet ($m)	Blue Chip's share of the cash dividend paid by Mutual Savings during the year ($m)	Annual return on Blue Chip's equity from the Mutual Savings dividend (%)
1975	12.0	1.9	16.1
1976	20.6	3.2	15.7
1977	23.9	3.8	16.1
1978	25.3	5.3	20.9
1979	25.6	6.7	26.3
1980	22.4	9.9	44.0
1981	18.8	1.9	10.2

Source: Charles T. Munger and Donald A. Koeppel, Blue Chip Stamps chairman and president's letter (1981)

With the money retained in Wesco, Louis Vincenti did a great job of guiding the rump Mutual Savings business. Munger and Buffett heaped praise on him. As well as getting good returns in the efficient, low-cost S&L, he was doing something alien to many empire-conscious managers; he was gradually shrinking his business. This was all for the sake of greater shareholder returns. Up to the point when Vincenti retired in 1983, Mutual made annual profits of more than $3m at a time when most other S&Ls were losing money.

But the S&L business was gradually demoted as better opportunities for capital use were seen elsewhere. By the late 1990s, the S&L business was referred to in Wesco's letter from Charlie Munger under the ignominious heading of "Tag Ends from Savings and Loan Days".

A very big tag end

While the original mortgage-providing S&L became a shadow of its former self, there was one tag end of that business that became worth hundreds of millions of dollars. Mutual had invested in 28,800,000 shares of Federal Home Loan Mortgage Corporation (Freddie Mac), for $72m. These were sold in 2000, "giving rise to the principal portion of the $852.4 million of after-tax securities gains realized by Wesco in 2000".[118]

When we consider that the whole of Wesco was valued at under $40m in the mid-1970s, if the $800m or so collected from Freddie Mac shares was all that the company comprised of in 2000, then we might have been satisfied with that return alone. But, there was much, much more to Wesco by then.

Wesco's insurance operations

The most important shift in Wesco's capital allocation came about in 1985. It started with a deal with Fireman's Fund. This former subsidiary of American Express floated on the stock exchange under the leadership of insurance company veteran Jack Byrne in 1985. Byrne had earned Buffett's undying admiration and gratitude for turning around GEICO, which had been on the verge of bankruptcy when Berkshire Hathaway took a major stake in the early 1970s (see Investment 2).

Buffett respected Byrne to such an extent that he signed up National Indemnity for 7% of all the insurance business in force at Fireman's Fund (with a few exceptions) for four years. This type of deal in the insurance world is called a quota-share contract. It means that Berkshire Hathaway's losses and costs on insurance companies were proportionate to the Fireman's Fund throughout the contract period.

In return, Fireman's Fund sent premiums to National Indemnity more or less as they came in. Thus the premium funds generated by accepting 7% of the risks were held within BH. This money was added to BH's float and could be invested. At that time, Fireman's Fund brought in about $3bn a year (expected to rise over the years). Thus around 7% of $3,000m ($210m) would flow to BH. Of course, as insurance claims arose money would flow the other way, but that would still have left a substantial float for Buffett to invest, given the often lengthy time delays between a policyholder paying a premium and claiming for an event.

In his 1985 letter, Buffett laid out the initial sums: "The company's [Fireman's Fund] September 1, 1985 unearned premium reserve was $1.324 billion, and it therefore transferred 7% of this, or $92.7 million, to us at initiation of the contract. We concurrently paid them $29.4 million representing the underwriting expenses that they had incurred on the transferred premium."[119]

Where did Wesco fit in?

While all the Fireman's Fund insurance was written by National Indemnity, two-sevenths of it was passed along to Wesco-Financial Insurance Company (Wes-FIC), a newly created insurance and reinsurance company (insuring insurers) subsidiary.

The agreement with Fireman's Fund to take premiums into Wesco came to an end in August 1989, but the benefit to Wesco continued. Tens of millions of dollars were left in Wes-FIC as a float to cover future claims for the premiums paid in the 1985–89 period. Even as late as 1997, $27.5m was retained in Wes-FIC as a reserve.

Charlie Munger knew very well the benefit of the money being held in reserve. As he said in his 1997 letter to Wesco shareholders, "it will take a long time before all claims are settled, and, meanwhile, Wes-FIC is being helped over many years by proceeds from investing 'float'."

Wes-FIC continued to take other reinsurance business, including large and small quota share arrangements similar and dissimilar to the reinsurance contract with Fireman's Fund Group. It wasn't long before the headquarters for Wes-FIC was Omaha, the epicentre of BH's insurance operations, despite the fact that it remained a Wesco subsidiary. After 1994, Wes-FIC extended its activities into a particular type of reinsurance, catastrophe-related insurance, called *super-cat* (earthquakes, hurricanes, etc.). This business required a large net worth relative to annual premiums received, because it had to withstand some enormous claims. Charlie Munger expressed the reason for being in this business as follows:

> "...super-cat reinsurance is not for the faint of heart. A huge variation in annual results, with some very unpleasant future years for Wes-FIC, is inevitable. But it is precisely what must, in the nature of things, be associated with these bad possibilities, with their huge and embarrassing adverse consequences in occasional years, that makes Wes-FIC like its way of being in the super-cat business. Buyers (particularly wise buyers) of super-cat reinsurance often want to deal with Berkshire Hathaway subsidiaries (possessing as they do the highest possible credit ratings and a reliable corporate personality) instead of other reinsurers less cautious, straightforward and well endowed... Thus the forces in place can rationally be expected to cause acceptable long-term results for well-financed, disciplined decision makers, despite horrible losses in some years and other years of restricted opportunity to write business... Wes-FIC, in the arrangements with... Berkshire Hathaway, receives a special business-acquisition advantage from using Berkshire Hathaway's general reputation."[120]

Standard and Poor's was so impressed with Wesco that it assigned it the highest possible claims-paying-ability rating: AAA. Wesco by this time had very large sums of money invested in securities (such as Freddie Mac) left over from the contracting S&L business. It also had a reputational advantage from its association with Berkshire Hathaway.

Because of the relationship between Wesco and BH, based on mutual trust, and the extraordinary expertise of BH's insurance underwriters, the board of Wesco approved the automatic taking of reinsurance risk offered by one or more wholly-owned Berkshire Hathaway subsidiaries. The beauty of this arrangement was that Wes-FIC needed very few staff and therefore had very low costs – it had virtually no insurance-acquisition or insurance administration costs.

Unfortunately the super-cat business produced poor underwriting profits. In fact, all the early profits made in that area were more than wiped out by the $10m or more lost on the Twin Towers attack in 2001. But at least Wes-FIC had the use of float created by the super-cat business to add to the much larger float generated from the more significant reinsurance deals; this was mostly focused on aviation, ship hull, liability and workers' compensation exposures.

The net income for West-FIC in those years (where such income was separated from BH's data) is shown in Table 22.2. This is largely investment income rather than underwriting income, because Wes-FIC's underwriting losses for reinsurance in bad years tended to offset underwriting gains in good years.

Note that to produce this level of interest and dividend income (capital gains on realised assets such as the Freddie Mac investment are recorded separately) required hundreds of millions of dollars in debt, preferred and equity securities – clearly Wesco had grown very big by the 1990s.

Table 22.2: Wes-FIC net income (interest and dividends on securities plus underwriting profit or loss)

Year	$m
1996	25.0
1997	27.5
1998	29.5
1999	37.2
2000	38.6
2001	35.9
2002	42.0
2003	40.1
2004	35.7
2005	42.8
2006	55.4
2007	61.3
2008	62.8

The mini-conglomerate

The year 1996 saw Wesco advance further into insurance with the purchase of Kansas Bankers Surety (KBS) for approximately $80m in cash. The following year KBS contributed $6m to the net operating income of the insurance businesses. This may not seem a great return on the $80m, but Buffett and Munger reckoned it had such good economics with an excellent underwriting record, and an outstanding manager, that KBS would soon contribute a lot more.

The Kansas Bankers Surety business

KBS started in 1909 as an underwriter of deposit insurance for Kansas banks. This means that it insured money deposited in a bank, guaranteeing that it would be returned to the depositor even in the event of a bank closure (the amount beyond that covered by the federal government). Over the years, it expanded to include small and medium-sized community banks spread through 22 mainly Midwestern states. It also offered policies which paid out if the directors and managers of the banks became publically liable for misdeeds or similar (directors and officers indemnity policies). Premiums were also charged for bank employment practices policies, bank annuity and mutual funds indemnity policies, and bank insurance agents professional errors and omissions indemnity policies. Being entirely focused on a subset of banks, and being so recognised and knowledgeable in that field, gave KBS a competitive advantage.

The key person Buffett and Munger identified at KBS was Donald Towle, the president. He had a great knowledge of this niche market and ran a tight ship assisted by only 13 officers and employees. In his 1996 BH letter, Buffett called Towle "an extraordinary manager. Don has developed first-hand relationships with hundreds of bankers and knows every detail of his operation. He thinks of himself as running a company that is 'his', an attitude we treasure at Berkshire."

In the 1996 BH letter, Buffett poked fun at himself for the supposed haphazard way in which he had selected this business for purchase:

> "You might be interested in the carefully-crafted and sophisticated acquisition strategy that allowed Berkshire to nab this deal. Early in 1996 I was invited to the 40th birthday party of my nephew's wife, Jane Rogers. My taste for social events being low, I immediately, and in my standard, gracious way, began to invent reasons for skipping

the event. The party planners then countered brilliantly by offering me a seat next to a man I always enjoy, Jane's dad, Roy Dinsdale – so I went.

The party took place on January 26. Though the music was loud – Why must bands play as if they will be paid by the decibel? – I just managed to hear Roy say he'd come from a directors meeting at Kansas Bankers Surety, a company I'd always admired. I shouted back that he should let me know if it ever became available for purchase.

On February 12, I got the following letter from Roy: 'Dear Warren: Enclosed is the annual financial information on Kansas Bankers Surety. This is the company that we talked about at Janie's party. If I can be of any further help, please let me know.' On February 13, I told Roy we would pay $75 million for the company – and before long we had a deal. I'm now scheming to get invited to Jane's next party."[121]

The already strong market position of KBS was enhanced by the BH association. Don Towle said that being part of Berkshire meant that no one questioned KBS' ability to pay out on claims. He also said that Buffett was very good at simply letting the company grow without interference. Today KBS is still run by a very small team, still very focused on insuring banks and still headquartered in Kansas.

CORT Business Services

Wesco bought into the business of renting furniture for placing in offices and apartments by buying CORT Business Services in February 2000, paying $384m in cash. The key ingredients of so many Buffett and Munger purchases were there: a good business in an unglamorous, overlooked sector, and therefore not overpriced; and an outstanding manager, Paul Arnold.

CORT was the national leader in its business area, with 117 showrooms, and was on the rebound from an aborted leveraged buyout. In 1999, total revenues were $354m. Of this, $295m was furniture rental revenue and $59m was furniture sales revenue. Before-tax profits in 1999 were $46m. Most large US companies rented from CORT when they needed temporary furnishings. Generally, when the furniture has been rented out three times it is sold off at CORT's clearance centres.

From the outset Paul Arnold was guaranteed "no interference from Wesco headquarters. We would be crazy to second-guess a man with his record in business."[122] Munger also expressed his expectation that there would be a "considerable expansion" of this business.

A very long-term focus

Despite their initial optimism, Buffett and Munger had to be very patient with this one – in fact, they are still waiting today for a good return. Demand for office furniture slumped after the dotcom bust of 2000 and the events of 11 September 2001. Whereas operating income had been $29m in the ten months from March to December 2000, it slid to less than half that in 2001, at $13.1m, and to losses in 2003.

Munger ruefully reflected in his 2001 letter on the difficulty for even the most able and experienced investors to predict economic and other events: "Obviously, when we purchased CORT we were poor predictors of near-term industry-wide prospects of the 'rent-to-rent' sector of the furniture business." Despite the hard times, CORT added to its geographical reach by buying some small US companies in the same field during the recession. It also built up its apartment-search wing, helping corporations to relocate staff.

After three years or so things started to gradually turn around and by 2006 after-tax profit was almost back to the level of 2000, at $26.9m. But then along came the 2009 financial crisis slump, sending CORT into the red again. Profits (in the form of pre-tax earnings) have been gradually improving since then:

- 2011: $29m

- 2012: $42m

- 2013: $42m

- 2014: $49m

- 2015: $55m

Despite the recent profit lift, you have to question whether the price of $384m to buy this company had enough margin of safety built-in. Perhaps it will improve from this point.

The merger is completed, after 35 years

At last, in 2011, the 19.9% of Wesco shares not owned by Berkshire Hathaway were bought from the other shareholders. The cost was $550m. Multiplying by five gives us a valuation of Wesco at that time of $2.75bn. Not a bad return on the $30m–$40m paid for 80% of Wesco by Blue Chip Stamps.

Where did this value come from? After all, Precision Steel did not contribute much, nor did CORT. The secret was in the use of the original capital tied up in the S&L business. This was gradually moved into bonds, preferred stock and equities within the original Wesco, resulting in some excellent investments such as Freddie Mac, which rose from $72m to over $800m.

Then, Wesco developed its reinsurance and banking insurance businesses, both piggybacking on Berkshire Hathaway's underwriting expertise, but having its own pile of money as insurance float available for investment in securities. Many of these did very well. Three examples were:

- **Salomon and Travelers Group**: In 1997, Wesco agreed to exchange the preferred stock and common stock it held in

Salomon Inc., which had cost $80m ten years earlier, for preferred and common shares in Travelers Group. These Travelers shares were worth about $112.1m more than Wesco paid for its Salomon stake, giving a 140% return.

- **Gillette and Procter & Gamble**: Convertible stock in Gillette, which cost $40m in 1989, was converted into common stock in 1991. This was exchanged in 2005 for $216.1m shares in Procter & Gamble, for a 440% return.

- **Wells Fargo**: This 2008 investment was not the best timed, but notwithstanding the Great Recession, Wells Fargo shares rose from $26 in January 2008 to $44 today.

Learning points

1. **Treat your reputation as a highly important asset.** If Betty Peters had not been impressed by Buffett's reputation before she agreed to meet him this deal would not have gone ahead.

2. **Mistakes in capital allocation will be made, such as with Precision Steel.** Good investors/managers have resilience to hits of this kind and press forward regardless with sound principles.

3. **Watch for downside risk.** If industry leaders are running towards a cliff-edge in fashion-induced collective wrong-headedness, as with the S&Ls in the 1980s with fixed mortgage rates combined with floating deposit rates, or the banks in 2007 buying securitised bonds, then investors need to position themselves to reduce the losses if/when it all collapses.

4. **Trust brings large savings.** For example, Wesco could trust Berkshire's insurance underwriters to bring in sensibly priced insurance policies, thus saving it from paying for an expensive underwriting team of its own.

Consolidation

EVERYTHING INTO
BERKSHIRE HATHAWAY

We now come to a very significant turning point in the career of Warren Buffett. In the mid-1970s, he was worth about £100m, but his funds were spread between investment vehicles. Some in a personal portfolio, some in Berkshire Hathaway, some in Diversified Retailing Company and some in Blue Chip Stamps. To confuse things further, these organisation held shares in each other. And each had its own collection of outside shareholders, with their individual interests.

After more than 30 years of investing, Buffett was pushed to bring clarity to the ownership structure. This chapter tells the story of the consolidation.

The tangle

In the mid-1970s, Buffett's direct shareholdings and the cross-holdings of the various companies changed from time to time, but the broad picture remained much the same until the Great Consolidation came about. To express precise percentages would only present a confusing picture and so, given the state of flux of holdings during those three or four years, I've greatly simplified the situation to provide only very rough fractions owned by each party. This is illustrated in the diagram below.

Approximate shareholdings in mid-1970s

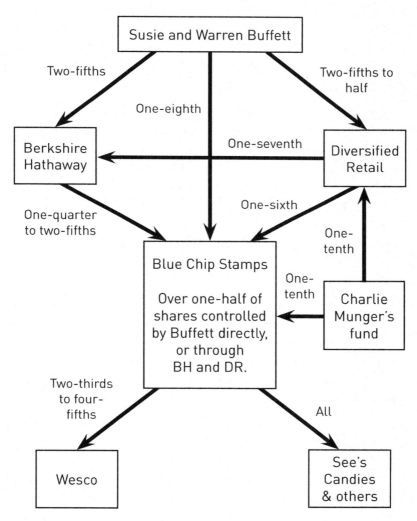

The authorities took an interest

In 1974, the Securities and Exchange Commission (SEC) noticed the Wesco dealings. They were concerned that Buffett and Munger owned shares in Blue Chip, both directly and via Diversified Retailing. Also Buffett influenced Blue Chip through Berkshire Hathaway. (At this stage Munger had no share stake in BH, nor a managerial position.) Furthermore, Buffett could command around one-half of Berkshire either through a personal shareholding or via the BH shares held by Diversified.

On the face of it, there was significant potential for conflicts of interest. After all, each of these companies had other shareholders. In unscrupulous hands this amount of power could be used against those shareholders. One of the questions the SEC was bound to ask was whether Munger and Buffett conspired to manipulate share prices of target companies? A particular area for attention was the relationship with Munger's fund and the control of Blue Chip, and its control of firms such as Wesco. *Where did the minority shareholders stand here?*

Justifying their actions

Buffett was already aware that the structure of his shareholdings was unnecessarily complicated and that an outsider could be suspicious that the interests of minority shareholders might be prejudiced. Thus he announced a plan to merge Diversified Retail into Berkshire Hathaway.

The SEC, ever leery, wanted to know what was going on – they had a lot of questions. Munger and Buffett explained the motivation and the many details in the fall of 1974. Then, to their great annoyance, the SEC announced a formal investigation, "In the Matter of Blue Chip Stamps, Berkshire Hathaway Incorporated, Warren Buffet [sic] HO-784". The SEC was to examine if Buffett had, on his own or in concert with others, devised and worked a scheme to defraud, and whether he had lied or omitted a material fact. Had Blue Chip manipulated Wesco's share price? What other games had Buffett and Munger cooked up?

Vast quantities of documents concerning Berkshire, See's and all the other companies were sent to the SEC. In March 1975, Munger and Buffett were summoned for two days of testimony.

Q. Had Munger shorted the shares of Santa Barbara Savings and Loan?

Answer: No.

Q. Had Blue Chip worked to stop the Wesco-Santa Barbara merger in order to buy it for itself without declaring its intention to merge?

Answer: It was not a definite plan to merge, only a remote possibility.

Q. Why pay over the odds for the Wesco shares after the merger deal had fallen through; after all, Blue Chip shareholders lose that way, don't they?

Answer: In the long run Blue Chip shareholders will do better if its directors act fairly toward Wesco shareholders, retaining the goodwill of Louis Vincenti, Betty Peters and others at Wesco. Relationships after acquisition matter a great deal.

Buffett's great consolidation

The SEC investigations into the tangle of Buffett's holdings and his and Munger's actions at Blue Chip and Wesco dragged on through 1975. Clearly, the complexity of the Buffett investment structure had exacerbated the situation by opening them to deepening suspicion that something nefarious was going on. Buffett became increasingly determined to simplify his businesses.

Two years after the inquiry began a judgement was given: Blue Chip had set out to defeat the merger and had artificially inflated

Wesco's share price. Despite this, no action was taken against Buffett. A promise was made not to do it again. Without any admission or denial of guilt, Blue Chip paid $115,000 to some Wesco shareholders who were supposedly hurt by the actions. In all, it was not much more than a slap on the wrist.

The merger

Finally, in 1978, Diversified Retail, which was by then both a retailer and a fire, casualty and workers' compensation insurance business, was merged into Berkshire. In return for Munger's Diversified shares he was given a 2% stake in Berkshire and made vice chairman (he had already closed his investment partnership).

Sandy Gottesman, as one of the shareholders of Diversified, ended up with a slightly lower percentage of Berkshire than Munger.

Now Berkshire controlled Blue Chip through a majority stake (about 58%) and Buffett had virtually no share portfolio outside of Berkshire other than a 13% stake in Blue Chip. He held 43%, and Susie Buffett 3%, of Berkshire Hathaway. In 1983, Berkshire bought all the remaining shares in Blue Chip to complete the clean-up.

A time for reflection

Aged 48, when he had completed the merger of Diversified with Berkshire, Buffett could look at his creation with immense satisfaction. The shares quickly rose above $200 each, meaning that Buffett and his wife were worth over $100m.

Buffett had grown from an 11-year-old investing in six preferred shares of Capital Cities for his sister Doris and himself, with only $229.50, to being in charge of a business empire that benefited from glorious assets, such as See's Candies, that pumped out millions of dollars for him to invest elsewhere.

He also controlled hundreds of millions of dollars in insurance floats to invest year after year and could, in most years, rely on an underwriting profit to boot. Even better, he had stakes in wonderful corporations, run by wonderful people whose camaraderie he enjoyed, such as Kay Graham at *Washington Post* and Gene Abegg at Illinois National Bank. No wonder he tap-danced his way to work every day.

Buffett was no longer fearful of poverty; he had built a significant buffer. So what was driving him to go on? Like so many multi-millionaires continuing to work extraordinarily hard, he loved the thrill of the game, the painting of the unfinished canvas. He was a creative and he wanted to go on using his brain to produce something bigger, better, greater. With the solid foundation of Berkshire Hathaway, he could really build something magnificent. Over the next four decades, he turned this one-time frail textile mill operator into one of the top five stock market companies in the world, worth over $400bn. He now controls influential stakes in Coca-Cola, Wells Fargo, Burlington North Santa Fe, American Express, IBM and a host of others.

More than that, Buffett is still growing the empire. If he lives a few more years I see no reason why he won't come to be at the head of the largest non-government controlled business in the world. Not bad for a humble lad from Omaha, who always followed the dictum of don't do anything you would not want reported on the front page of your local newspaper by an objective reporter, for your spouse, relatives and friend to read the next day.

Appendix – Deal Summary

This appendix presents a summary table of the investment deals described in volume 1. The information in the table is largely drawn from the deal summary boxes at the start of each chapter.

Deal	Date		Value ($)		Profit ($)
	Bought	Sold	Bought	Sold	
Cities Services	1941	1941	114.75	120	5.25
GEICO	1951	1952	10,282	15,259	4,977
Rockwood & Co.	1954	1955	Various	Various	13,000
Dempster Mill	1956	1963	999,600	3.3m	2.3m
Sanborn Maps	1958	1960	About 1m	Exchanged for portfolio of shares	Roughly 50%
Berkshire Hathaway (BH)	1962	N/A	14.86 per share	Trading today at 245,000 per share	Billions
American Express	1964	1968	13m	33m	20m
Disney	1966	1967	4.0m	6.2m	2.2m
Hochschild-Kohn	1966	1969	4.8m	4.0m	–0.8m
National Indemnity Insurance	1967	N/A	8.6m	N/A	Billions
Associated Cotton Shops	1967	N/A	6m	Merged with BH in 1970s	Unknown

Deal	Date		Value ($)		Profit ($)
	Bought	Sold	Bought	Sold	
Blue Chip Stamps	1968	N/A	3m–4m	Now part of BH	Hundreds of millions
Illinois National Bank and Trust	1969	1980	15.5m	17.5m	>32m (including dividends)
Omaha Sun Newspapers	1969	1980	1.25	Unknown	Unknown, but a loss
See's Candies	1972	N/A	25m	Now part of BH	>2bn
Washington Post	1974	N/A	10.6m	Exchanged for a portfolio of businesses	Hundreds of millions
Wesco Financial	1974	N/A	30m–40m	Now part of BH	>2bn

Notes on the table

- Figures in the table are the most accurate available. In some cases it was necessary to make estimates based upon information taken from a range of sources.

- Where N/A is stated for the sale date, in most cases this means Buffett never sold the company and still holds it today within Berkshire Hathaway.

- The dollar amounts in the 'Value ($)' column are the absolute amounts bought and sold in each transaction.

Endnotes

1. Benjamin Graham and David Dodd, *Security Analysis* (Whittlesey House, McGraw-Hill, 1934).
2. Ibid., Chapter 2.
3. Warren Buffett, speech at New York Society of Security Analysts (6 December 1994).
4. Warren Buffett, BPL letter to partners (1959).
5. Warren Buffett, BPL letter to partners (1958).
6. Warren Buffett, BPL letter to partners (1961).
7. Warren Buffett, BPL letter to partners (1963).
8. Andrew Kilpatrick, *Of Permanent Value: The Story of Warren Buffett* (Southern Publishers Group, 1996), p. 139.
9. Ibid., p.139.
10. Warren Buffett, BPL letter to partners (1964).
11. Warren Buffett, BPL letter to partners (1963).
12. I devote a chapter to Fisher in both *The Financial Times to Value Investing* and *The Great Investors*. You might also consider reading Fisher's book, *Common Stocks and Uncommon Profits*.
13. A more detailed explanation of the PE is beyond the scope of this book, but there are many useful resources on the internet if you wish to learn more. Just type 'price-to-earnings ratio PE' into a search engine.
14. Warren Buffett, letter to shareholders of BH (1995).
15. Warren Buffett, lecture at the University of Notre Dame, www.tilsonfunds.com/BuffettNotreDame.pdf (1991).
16. Warren Buffett, letter to shareholders of BH (1995).
17. Warren Buffett, letter to shareholders of BH (1989).
18. Warren Buffett, letter to shareholders of BH (2014).
19. Ibid.
20. Warren Buffett, letter to shareholders of BH (1966).
21. Warren Buffett, letter to shareholders of BH (2014).

22. Roger Lowenstein, *Buffett: The Making of an American Capitalist* (Broadway Books, New York, 1995).

23. Jack Ringwalt's memoir, *Tales of National Indemnity and Its Founder Jack D. Ringwalt*.

24. Ibid.

25. Ibid.

26. Ibid.

27. Warren Buffett, letter to shareholders of BH (2014).

28. Warren Buffett, BPL letter to partners (1968).

29. Quoted in Alice Schroeder, *The Snowball: Warren Buffett and the Business of Life* (Bloomsbury, 2009). pp. 252–3.

30. Warren Buffett, letter to shareholders of BH (1989).

31. Warren Buffett, BPL letter to partners (January 1969).

32. Warren Buffett, BPL letter to partners (December 1969)

33. Warren Buffett, BPL letter to partners (January 1966).

34. Warren Buffett, BPL letter to partners (July 1966).

35. Warren Buffett, BPL letter to partners (January 1967).

36. Ibid.

37. Ibid.

38. Ibid.

39. Ibid.

40. Ibid.

41. Ibid.

42. Ibid.

43. Warren Buffett, BPL letter to partners (October 1967).

44. Ibid.

45. Ibid.

46. Warren Buffett, BPL letter to partners (October 1967).

47. Ibid.

48. Ibid.

49. Ibid.

50. Ibid.

51. Warren Buffett, BPL letter to partners (January 1968).

52. Ibid.

53. Ibid.

54. Ken Chace, letter to shareholders of BH (1967).

55. Warren Buffett, letter to shareholders of BH (2001).

56. Warren Buffett, letter to shareholders of BH (1978).

57. Warren Buffett, letter to shareholders of BH (1975).

58. Warren Buffett, letter to shareholders of BH (1979).
59. Ibid.
60. Warren Buffett, letter to shareholders of BH (1980).
61. Warren Buffett, letter to shareholders of BH (1982).
62. Warren Buffett, BPL letter to partners (July 1968).
63. Ibid.
64. Ibid.
65. *Buffalo News*, 21 December 2012.
66. Ken Chace, President's letter to shareholders of BH (April 1970).
67. Ibid.
68. Ibid.
69. Warren Buffett, BPL letter to partners (December 1969).
70. Ibid.
71. Quoted by Warren Buffett, BPL letter to partners (January 1969).
72. Ibid.
73. Ibid.
74. Ibid.
75. Warren Buffett, BPL letter to partners (May 1969).
76. Ibid.
77. Ibid.
78. Ibid.
79. Ibid.
80. Ibid.
81. Ibid.
82. Ibid.
83. Ibid.
84. Reproduced in Benjamin Graham, *The Intelligent Investor* (Harper Business Essentials, 1973).
85. Warren Buffett, BPL letter to partners (October 1969).
86. Ibid.
87. Ibid.
88. Ibid.
89. Ibid.
90. Ibid.
91. Ibid.
92. Warren Buffett, BPL letter to partners (December 1969).
93. Warren Buffett, letter to shareholders of BH (2006).
94. Daniel Roberts, 'The Secrets of See's Candies', *Fortune* (3 September 2012).

95. Quoted in Carol Loomis, 'The Inside Story of Warren Buffett', *Fortune* (11 April 1988).
96. Warren Buffett, 'Warren Buffett Talks Business', Talk given to students at the University of North Carolina, Center for Public Television, Chapel Hill (1995).
97. Warren Buffett, letter to shareholders of BH (2014)
98. Warren Buffett, letter to shareholders of BH (1999).
99. Warren Buffett, letter to shareholders of BH (2014).
100. Warren Buffett, letter to shareholders of BH (2011).
101. Warren Buffett, letter to shareholders of BH (1999).
102. Warren Buffett, letter to shareholders of BH (2014).
103. Warren Buffett, letter to shareholders of BH (1973).
104. Warren Buffett, letter to shareholders of BH (1973).
105. Ibid.
106. Anthony Simpson, 'Look At All Those Beautiful, Scantily Clad Girls Out There!', *Forbes* (1 November 1974).
107. Ibid.
108. Warren Buffett, letter to shareholders of BH (1985).
109. Newsweek, 1972 annual report.
110. Warren Buffett, letter to shareholders of BH (1987).
111. Warren Buffett, letter to shareholders of BH (1985).
112. Ibid.
113. Having written the best-selling UK university textbook on corporate finance I must take some of the blame. But at least I go on to explain that while the theories are interesting and have their uses, there are many real-world complications which mean that we have to proceed cautiously in application.
114. Warren Buffett, letter to shareholders of BH (1986).
115. Jerry Goodman ('Adam Smith'), *Supermoney* (1972).
116. The shares were bought at various prices over a long period.
117. Charles Munger and Donald Koeppel, Blue Chip Stamps letter to shareholders (1977).
118. Charles Munger, letter to Wesco shareholders (2000).
119. Warren Buffett, letter to shareholders of BH (1985).
120. Charles Munger, Chairman's letter to Wesco shareholders (1997).
121. Warren Buffett, letter to shareholders of BH (1996).
122. Charles Munger, letter to Wesco shareholders (1999).

Index

Note: Page numbers in *italic* refer to figures, page numbers in **bold** refer to charts or tables.

CPSIA information can be obtained
at www.ICGtesting.com
Printed in the USA
BVOW09*0052151217
502577BV00001B/2/P